Who's the BOSS?

The Win-Win Way to Parent Your Defiant Strong-Willed Child

Don MacMannis, Ph.D.
Debra Manchester MacMannis, M.S.W.

ISBN-13: 978-1502550422
ISBN-10: 1502550423

Distributed by Create Space

Cover Design by Jen Brookman

Printed in the United States of America

Table of Contents

INTRODUCTION

If the home is to be a means of grace, it must be a place of rules. The alternative to rule is not freedom, but the unconstitutional tyranny of the most selfish member.
-C.S. Lewis

*S*ara, a precocious four-year-old, came with her parents for their first counseling session. Her preschool teacher suggested they get some help for Sara's emotional outbursts. She had even gotten in trouble for biting other kids when she didn't get her way. Her teacher really liked Sara but was concerned about her behavior. The parents were embarrassed and completely at a loss.

Midway through the first session, we asked Sara, "Who's the boss in your family?" She pointed to her dad. Her mom burst into fit of laughter, exclaiming, "That's so not true." Sara started to giggle, then threw her hands on her hips and proclaimed "Mommy's right. I'm the boss! But she wants to be the boss and that's why we're here."

DOES THIS SOUND AT ALL FAMILIAR?

Perhaps you can relate to some of these other real-life cases:

- A six-year-old boy who's a bundle of energy rarely responds to his parents' requests and expects conversations and attention to revolve around him at the cost of other family members.
- A seven-year-old girl gets to decide when she goes to bed, who reads her a story at night, and if or when she brushes her teeth (or not).
- A nine-year-old is deeply unhappy because he can't make or keep friends. In the classroom, he smacks kids in the back of the head to get attention.
- A four-year old child throws a temper tantrum every time she goes to the grocery store and doesn't get the treat she wants.

Ask yourself the following questions about your parenting:

- Do you have to raise your voice, lecture or repeat yourself to get your kids to behave?
- Do your kids ignore normal, everyday requests when they just don't feel like listening?
- Have you tried tons of different approaches to no avail?
- Have you been trying to avoid spanking and yelling but nothing else seems to work?
- Are you exhausted and upset because your kids seem disrespectful, entitled or ungrateful for all the things you do for them?
- Are you feeling frustrated and defeated despite your best efforts to be a great parent?

If you ever used the words strong-willed, defiant, spoiled, entitled, overly demanding, won't listen, difficult or out of control or if you answered yes to some or all of the questions above, welcome to the club. Millions of parents are struggling, like you, with kids that are spiraling out of control—kids who need to learn how to listen better, comply to normal everyday requests, and take no for an answer.

The good news is we've helped hundreds of parents overcome these challenges and become successful, thriving, loving families. So read on....there's hope!

In our respective roles as child psychologist and clinical social worker, we have been counseling kids and parents day in and day out and co-directing a non-profit family therapy clinic for well over thirty years. As a father and mother of two grown sons, we have experienced first hand the trials and tribulations of parenthood. As a married dual career couple, we have faced the challenges of sharing leadership in a family, working together as a team, and balancing the demands of work and home. In short, we have learned most of what we will share with you while deep in the trenches with thousands of families from diverse backgrounds—socio-economic, cultural, racial, sexual orientation, religious or not, single parented and blended.

Our goal is simple, namely, to help children feel good about themselves <u>and</u> have love and respect for others. We know from years of experience backed by solid research that children who have too much power over their parents are at risk for a host of problems. Kids who act and are treated like they are the boss of the family not only drive their parents crazy but often get in trouble in school, have difficulty with peers, and are deprived of fundamental lessons needed to survive in a world that will not always revolve around them.

HOW DO WE DEFINE A STRONG-WILLED CHILD?

Every child is unique—born with particular physical, emotional, and intellectual characteristics and capacities. There is no one gene that causes some children to be more willful than others, which means that even so-called strong-willed children are not all alike. (See Chapter 17 for in-depth discussion of the inborn aspects of a child's temperament.)

That being said, most parents know when they have one. Especially when parents have more than one child. Often highly intelligent and curious, some children are simply more difficult to control than others. They know what they want and protest loudly when they don't get it. They tend to be more emotional about everything, especially their wants and needs.

Susan and David brought their 5, 8 and 10-year-old children for a family session. The oldest and youngest both sat in their chairs as mom and dad had directed. Sam, the middle child, ignored their multiple requests for him to sit down, whereupon he picked up a puppet without asking and began to tickle his 5-year-old sister. The parents shared that he was often defiant at home and that the teacher had referred them to our clinic because of Sam's disruptiveness in class. His parents knew without asking that he was strong-willed. Little did they know how much this behavior could shift in a short period of time.

WHAT'S UP WITH FAMILIES THESE DAYS?

Family researchers have known for years that healthy families create environments that balance large doses of love and warmth with sufficient firmness and structure. Kids thrive in these settings. Without love and warmth they tend to feel abandoned and resentful, and without firmness and structure they will often become anxious and/or have behavior problems. This core concept has not changed and is not likely to do so.

That being said, the world has undergone tremendous changes in the past twenty-five years. Many of today's parents and their kids have no memory of life without the Internet. In 1995, only 3% of Americans went on-line. Now 97% of people ages 18-29 and 99% of individuals in households earning $75,000 or more have integrated computer usage into their daily life.

The implications for families of this dramatic shift in available information, constantly at their fingertips, are being examined and discussed in the news and confronted in counseling offices. Issues confronting parents around kids' use of cell phones, computers, social network sites, videogames, and Internet safety are new arenas that demand structure, rules and guidance. (We devoted a whole section to this topic in Chapter 6.) The stakes are getting higher. Kids so desperately need established rules and limits as they grow up in an increasingly complex world.

The Internet brings not only helpful information but inundates children with advertising. E-commerce sales now top $1 trillion worldwide and social network sites aim their advertising at younger and younger children. It is more difficult but perhaps more important than ever that parents stem the tide of materialism and social pressures now bombarding kids. Although there have always been some parents who were too permissive, the relentless nature of the media now makes parenting more challenging than ever before.

Another reason more parents are struggling with out of control kids is due to increased economic stresses. As both mothers and fathers spend extra hours working outside the home, they have less time to be with their kids. The guilt stemming from this shortage of family time, and from divorce as well, often prompts parents to be more lenient—an understandable but unhelpful means of compensating.

> Sometimes a pattern of permissiveness develops when parents feel sorry for a child and proceed to allow inappropriate behavior. One mom realized in therapy that she had relaxed the rules too much with her eight-year-old daughter, Mattie, because of recent family traumas. The parents' divorce was immediately followed by the loss of their home in a wildfire. The child had lots of feelings about losing her family and all of her possessions, but was also acting out as a way of testing boundaries. Receiving more limits and structure dramatically helped to lessen Mattie's anxieties.

With information comes misinformation. When asked why they allow their children to wield so much power over them, many parents believe that discipline will injure their child's fragile self-esteem. In reality, letting children get away with too much—or overindulging them by giving them everything they want while not giving them responsibilities appropriate to their age and ability—can be as damaging to their feelings of self-worth as being too strict.

In a classic swing of the pendulum, many parents who consult with us are advocates of "attachment parenting." Forming a strong loving bond between parents and babies, known as a secure attachment, is an essential component of good parenting. But there is a big difference between nurturing behaviors and indulgence. Parents indulge kids when they do things for them that kids can do for themselves or by not saying "no" when appropriate. When kids have too much power, they become anxious about the impulses they cannot control, and as a result they feel bad about themselves and guilty about the pain they are causing.

Although being together as a family is important, the quantity of time devoted to it is not nearly as crucial as the quality of interactions and the methods of discipline we use. In most families where kids are misbehaving, the hierarchy is upside down with the kids wielding more power than their parents. Too much time is spent with kids in center stage, shuffling kids off to multiple activities, offering stimulation and entertainment to stave off boredom or misbehavior. Often, parents' guilt about too little quality time, time spent just talking and being together, results in more spoiling of the kids with gifts and gadgets and less insistence on helping out.

Overindulgence can also stem from parents' fears of making waves or being in conflict with their children. Some adults don't mind a good fight but others avoid conflict at all costs. This can be due to many factors—our temperament (more on this later), upbringing, cultural background or religious beliefs.

For some parents it's far too important to be their child's best friend. This is especially true when adults lack adequate social support from extended family or friends. Since a crucial part of parenting is being able to put your foot down now and then, you can't be dependent on your children's love and approval. It's essential not to have all of your emotional eggs in one basket. We have a favorite adage about this dilemma:

If your child isn't upset with you sometimes, you probably aren't setting enough limits.

Although parents should be in charge, this doesn't mean that they deserve respect but their children don't. Respect must flow in both directions in a win-win way. Children who feel respected and understood for their feelings, in turn, listen better to their parents— not like little robots or people pleasers, but also not like defiant insurrectionists.

No child can be expected to do exactly what mom or dad says the very first time they say something. Children are still children, and it is part of their nature to stretch limits, test, and experiment with the world around them. However, parents in healthy families know that they can enforce their requests, and when they really mean it, their child will comply.

WELCOME ABOARD

We assume that you, like many parents, want to build a closer, more cooperative relationship with one or more of your children. Or perhaps you are curious about how effective your parenting approach is when compared to others. It may very challenging if you were raised in a family with either inadequate boundaries or limits or, conversely, with overly harsh, punitive forms of punishment. Lacking healthy models, it is typical to parent haphazardly, often with too much emotion and not enough consistency or structure.

This book can help you find your bearings. We developed this approach while raising our own children and also while counseling thousands of families who turned to us for help. This book is dedicated to these families and to their lovable (though sometimes exasperating) strong-willed children.

WHEN TO START THIS NEW SYSTEM

Before you get started, we'd like to share a concern about the timing of your start. If you and your spouse or co-parenting partner are currently having high levels of conflict, you may want to attend to couple's issues first. An essential ingredient of effective parenting is that you be on the same page as your co-parenting partner(s).

There are a number of different facets of a strong parental and spousal team. Healthy relationships are formed when there is a strong bond of love and friendship, a sense of intimacy and connectedness, a common philosophy and approach to parenting and the ability to make decisions and follow through together on action plans.

If your relationship suffers primarily from your frustrations as parents, but you have a strong connection in other ways, then it makes sense to proceed ahead. It is hugely challenging to have a strong-willed child who is acting like the boss of the family and acting disrespectful. If this is the main issue that's driven you into conflict and craziness with your partner, you should proceed with the Win-Win Way described in the following pages. (There will be more discussion about teamwork in Chapter 14.)

If, however, you are in high conflict with your partner and don't feel like you will be able to follow through as a united, functional parenting team, we recommend that you temporarily put this book aside and work on your adult relationship first. Creating a strong team will help you to weather the inevitable storms of change. We often playfully tell couples that need some relationship repair to "get their act together before they take their show on the road."

Bill and Britney showed up for a first session gung ho to get parenting help for their strong-willed 7-year-old daughter. They had heard about our system and wanted the tools ASAP. By the end of the session, however, they realized that they weren't quite ready to work as a team. Bill admitted drinking too much and also insisted on being right all the time, and Britney withdrew from him and nagged a lot. After two couple's sessions, Bill practically crawled into the next session alone, barely able to walk. He had gone out drinking with some friends and got so plastered that he fell and hurt himself badly. Finally, after feeling the threat of losing his family, he broke down in tears asking for help with his drinking problem. This was a rocky, but great beginning. The couple was able to implement the Win-Win Way with their daughter five weeks later.

ASSESSING YOUR FAMILY

Before we wrote *Who's the Boss?*, we published a self-help book on healthy families entitled *How's Your Family Really Doing? 10 Keys to a Happy Loving Family.* The 10 Keys are well-researched building blocks of happy loving families. In general, our two books have been created as companions to one another.

How's Your Family… can help you learn about and work on challenging areas of concern in your family. Key #5 is all about who's in charge and whether or not you parent with appropriate limits and structure. In fact, we wrote *Who's the Boss?* as the practical guidebook for parents struggling with Key #5.

To direct our counseling efforts, we developed an assessment tool to help families determine their current strengths and weaknesses. It's called the Current Family Assessment. A copy of this self-help tool can be found in Appendix A. (If you prefer to have an 8 ½ x 11" printout, you can download it for free under "Forms" at Strong-WilledChild.com.) This process usually takes around ten minutes. It's not only quite eye opening, but many families find that it's quite fun to take, especially as family members share and compare responses.

If you didn't score well on Key #5 in the Current Family Assessment, the Win-Win approach is tailor-made for you. It will give you hands-on tools and procedures to set limits in a caring and effective way with your strong-willed child. Although the book often uses examples of parenting teams with moms and dads, it works with families with two moms, two dads, and couples with different cultural and religious backgrounds.

The other Key in the Current Family Assessment to pay attention to now is Key #10, "Parenting Together." Your answer to the questions on this key can help you to decide whether you are ready to start yet. As we have emphasized, whether you are married or not, teamwork and being on the same page are crucial to the success of your undertaking.

You may be able to address conflicts and upsets with your partner using communication tools offered in self-help books such as *How's Your Family*....(at HowsYourFamily.com) or turning to books in our annotated bibliography or Self-Help Resources section found at our website. Or you may need some professional help from a psychotherapist that specializes in couple's therapy. No matter what approach you employ, be sure that you feel like a team and you've got each other's back before you try to implement the Win-Win Way.

A BRIEF OVERVIEW OF THE BOOK

Although we know that you are eager to embark on a new, more effective form of parenting, we recommend strongly that you read through the entire book once before you try to implement this program. By doing so, you will understand WHY you need a new approach, WHAT the new approach entails, and HOW you will be implementing it. After an initial read-through, you will then want to go back and review in more depth the specific and practical tools that we outline. Here is an overview to guide you in your process:

In Chapters 1-3 of the book, we discuss the many reasons why kids misbehave in the first place and why a positive approach to parenting, creating a win-win for parent and child alike, works more effectively than a top down, win-lose model. We ask the reader to determine where and when the problems are arising—at home, at school, or across all settings. We look at how some kids—the so-called strong-willed ones—push back more than others.

In Chapter 4 we provide the philosophical underpinnings of the model and the most important guidelines for transforming all of our relationships—including parenting. The first step in our program is to learn how and why to reduce negative emotions—especially anger and anxiety. We're not bringing out the best in our kids when we parent out of anger or fear. Before you try to implement the whole program described in this book, practice the tools provided in Chapter 4. If you rush ahead too quickly without addressing and learning to manage strong negative feelings first, your efforts may fall flat.

Chapter 5 addresses the reasons why physical punishment as a primary means of parenting, although still very commonly used in families, is not optimal or effective in helping kids behave.

Chapter 6 highlights the importance of openly discussing and agreeing upon consistent family rules. Since it's such a hot topic today, there is a special section on rules for "screen time."

Chapters 7 and 8 explain how internal and external motivators can be helpful in different ways. We underscore the importance of increasing the number of positive interactions with your child. The 5:1 ratio that we describe has been replicated in studies of families, loving marriages, classrooms, and even workplaces. Positive expressions such as appreciations, praise, warmth, and playfulness are crucial to satisfaction in relationships.

Chapter 9 teaches the very specific use of the star chart to target the behaviors you are wishing to address with your child. Even if you have already heard of star charts, please read this chapter in detail. The big pay-off of dedicated parental attention is unique and crucial in our model. An engaging, playful aspect of the Win-Win program is when your kid gets to be "the boss" of you.

Chapters 10 and 11 present a unique form of time out as well as what to do if your child won't willingly cooperate with the program. Since a picture is worth a thousand words, we have provided links to video demos showing the way to explain and implement these procedures with love and care. We also describe how and why this form of time out and holding works and when it should not be used. Chapter 12 provides guidelines about when to start this program—and when not to— since it represents such a big change for the whole family.

Chapter 13 outlines the very specific way that we want you to introduce the nuts and bolts of the new program to the children in a pre-planned family meeting. This chapter, and the procedures described, are so important that we don't want you to start the new system without it. This initial meeting should also include any other adults who play a significant parenting role with your children.

Chapter 14 reveals two important roadblocks to change. The first is how unresolved issues from our past can surface in current relationships, unwittingly sabotaging our best efforts to change our style of parenting. We will urge you to complete the Current Family and Family of Origin Assessments to learn more about what triggers you and/or your partner. The second roadblock is when parents aren't on the same page when it comes to discipline.

Chapter 15 explains how sleep and exercise are essential in bringing out the best in kids. A high percentage of children with behavioral challenges are sleep deprived, inhibiting their ability to manage emotions. Regular aerobic exercise is also a highly effective tool for change.

Chapter 16 presents the unique challenges of various family forms such as stepfamilies and single parent households. It also outlines issues that arise during separation, divorce, and the blending of new families. Chapter 17 sheds light on the issues of temperament, special needs or learning styles, and mental illness.

In conclusion, making changes, even ones for the better, takes courage and commitment. Since you are reading this book, we figure that you are ready to examine how your parenting can be strengthened. Take your time, and try to enjoy the process. We've attempted to keep the book short and concise, but there's a lot to digest in the chapters that follow. Additional information can be found in the FAQs and blogs at our website.

CHAPTER ONE

THE WIN-WIN WAY

I came to parenting the way most of us do - knowing
nothing and trying to learn everything.
-Mayim Bialik

$\mathcal{T}$his approach is the result of over thirty-five years of study, research, teaching and clinical practice. It took years to develop and revise, lots through good old-fashioned trial and error. Hundreds of families with three to ten-year-old kids have successfully used the Win-Win Way to turn things around. Parents typically report dramatic improvement in kids' behavior after a mere two weeks time. Follow-up feedback from parents months and years later shows that improvements can be maintained by sticking with this approach.

This book is not intended to provide all of the essential elements of parenting. Rather, it describes a concise method and procedure for parents to turn things around and gain respect and cooperation from defiant, strong-willed children when things have gotten out of hand. Our previous title, *How's Your Family Really Doing?* is one of many resources for parents who need help in understanding and using tools to create a happy, loving family.

THE GOAL

The goal of this method of parenting is to form close relationships <u>and</u> to set limits with your kids in a way that maximizes their happiness and benefits the whole family. As you've probably noticed by now, one person's happiness or level of upset is bound to affect that of others as well. We are inextricably connected.

With this approach, your child can wind up being more loving, happy, less anxious, have a higher self-esteem and feel less guilty. At the same time as you strengthen your parental authority, you are helping your child learn to tolerate frustration, respect limits, and get along better with others. These social and emotional skills are crucial to your child's later success in life. Best of all, you can have more fun with your kids and leave behind the "bad cop" role, at least most of the time.

WHAT MAKES KIDS MISBEHAVE?

Kids misbehave for a variety of reasons. As you think about your own child's situation, keep in mind that it's usually a combination of many factors that influence their behavior, rather than just one explanation or another. It's best to not get concerned with how important one factor is compared to any other. Just figure out everything that might be contributing and attend accordingly.

Not in any order of importance, kids can misbehave because they are:

- Testing to see what they can get away with
- Not wanting to face frustration
- Wanting their parents' attention
- Showing their parents that they are upset
- Retaliating for feeling like they've been mistreated
- Expressing their anger or upset about anything going on in their lives
- Distracting their parents from their marital conflict
- Sacrificing themselves by drawing attention to their behavior and away from a parent(s) own struggles with stress, anxiety, depression, conflict, etc.
- Lacking sleep
- Hungry
- Suffering from ADD or other disorders with a genetic component

In our role as clinicians, we can never know the exact percentage of influence each of the above factors might have in any given case. But just by way of example, here's the pie chart that we think best reflects the causes for one child's misbehavior prior to successful treatment with our approach. Your child's influences might reflect a similar pattern, or quite a different one.

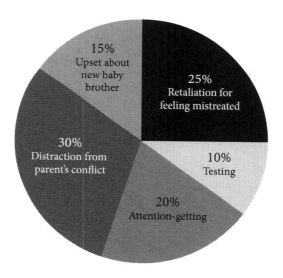

One of the most common challenges we face nowadays is with families where kids have been spoiled by all of the attention that they have received from well-meaning parents. Some children, having had one or both parents at their beck and call for years, act like they truly are the boss in the family. Their parents have become like slaves to their child's needs and demands, rarely expecting something back from their child in the way of reciprocation.

Nannies, baby-sitters, grandparents and family members in primary roles in a child's life can also overindulge kids to their detriment. They, too, should be involved with this new system of change and improvement.

The best way to discourage these negative behaviors is by working from a positive angle. This is accomplished with a lot of love and by supporting or reinforcing appropriate behavior. Whenever possible, you will devote time and attention to reinforcing positive actions, decreasing the level of conflict, increasing your child's self-esteem, and fostering warm feelings between family members.

WHAT MAKES THIS APPROACH UNIQUE?

- A child's willfulness becomes an asset instead of a liability.
- Kids become motivated to behave because they want to, not because of what you want.
- You will be given effective methods to reduce your own frustrations, thereby reducing negative emotions which fuel your child's behavior problems.
- You are given specific procedures to set limits in a caring and consistent manner.
- Steps are provided to ease the transition to the new set of rules, incentives and consequences.
- The discipline process itself teaches kids how to develop greater emotional "self-regulation."
- What kids earn by behaving is fun family time together. Nobody feels defeated. It's all win-win!

CHAPTER TWO

PROBLEMS AT SCHOOL AND/OR AT HOME

*If you do not change direction, you may end
up where you are heading.*
-Lao Tzu

*S*ome children have behavior problems that only surface at home, some only at school, and others in both settings. In the majority of cases, implementing this program at home is sufficient to affect school behavior as well. Children's home environments provide templates for how they behave elsewhere, so learning to respond to parental limits creates a process that gets internalized and then echoes into the school. There are some case exceptions that will be discussed in Chapter 17.

PROBLEMS MAKING OR KEEPING FRIENDS

As young children leave home and attend school, a primary source of their self-esteem comes from how peers relate to them. Children who aren't sufficiently connected to friends become unhappy, especially by third grade. All too frequently, kids who have problems responding to limits at home also have trouble making and keeping friends.

The reason? These kids haven't learned to be sufficiently attentive to others' needs. Simply put, they don't share very well. It's not just about sharing your cookie or taking turns, but something equally important—what we call "sharing influence." Because they have had too much power at home they tend to want to be in charge too much with their peers. This turns other kids off.

As children learn to be better behaved and less self-absorbed, then and only then can they interact with friends in ways where they share influence. Learning consideration for others allows them to say things like "How about let's do what you want first, and then I get to choose."

ACTING OUT ONLY IN SCHOOL

There are a number of reasons that kids can be acting out in school and not at home. Some factors relate to things that are happening at school, such as being bullied, socially isolated, or having special education needs that aren't being met.

Yet another explanation for kids' misbehavior in school is how things are going at home. There are two different patterns that are typical:

1. One pattern is that a child is being treated too punitively at home. Kids can be afraid of their parents, upset about how they are being disciplined, but instead of expressing their upset at home, they carry their anger and defiance into the classroom or playground. When parents are using spanking, yelling, or physical forms of punishment with strong emotion, kids often act out these same behaviors. This is a case of monkey see, monkey do.

2. Other kids may act out in school because there is too much tension in the family. Sometimes mom and dad are fighting, sleep deprived, or stressed out about work or health conditions. These children, especially sensitive ones, are typically acting out and expressing their stress and upset at school. The following case example illustrates this:

A mother and paternal grandmother were raising a seven-year-old girl named Grace. The friction in the room was palpable as these two parenting figures met in my office for the first time. They were at odds with each other about how and whether to set limits with Grace, who hadn't been completing homework, was getting into trouble with playground teasing, etc. It took a few sessions to help the adults work out their accumulation of upsets and resentments with each other. Then, and only then, could they team up and be on the same page about discipline. When the adults were able to collaborate and follow through with appropriate limits, Grace settled down.

Regardless of the specific family patterns that may be contributing to a child's misbehavior, the Win-Win Way is effective. As kids become less anxious and upset, they are less likely to act out in anger. They learn limits at home and their better behavior generalizes into the classroom. In a very caring fashion, you want your children to feel loved without giving them the message that they are the center of the universe.

CHAPTER THREE

WHO ARE THEY, ANYWAY?

*Loving a child doesn't mean giving in to all his whims; to love him is
to bring out the best in him, to teach him to love what is difficult.*
-Nadia Boulanger

*I*n previous generations, if children obeyed their parents, it was typically out of fear of a spanking (or worse), a guilt trip, a public shaming, or any number of aversive approaches. Congratulate yourself if you haven't had to resort to these old ways. But today's parents face a new dilemma. If your child isn't afraid of you and doesn't really care so much about what you think, you're in a bind. Now what do you do? You don't want to spank but don't have other strategies to replace the old ones. You may want to be more in charge but don't know how to get there from here.

As therapists, we get a high number of referrals of defiant, strong-willed children from pediatricians, teachers and principals. These kids already carry pretty heavy labels such as Oppositional Defiant Disorder and Bipolar Disorder. Parents will typically ask that their child be seen in individual therapy. Parents, and many professionals, as well, still haven't figured out that problems rarely exist only inside a child. It is the context of a child's life that can bring out the best or the worst. The primary context for young children is their home life— how they are being loved, cared for and disciplined.

This is why we work with parents from the outset. How can we "fix" a child without including the most important, powerful influences in that child's life? If you think about it, isn't it silly to imagine that an hour a week, even with an excellent therapist, will be more effective than changing the quality of a child's interactions at home? If after we teach parents this new approach, their kids change dramatically in a few weeks, is that because the disorder has been eradicated? Clearly not. The context in which the problem emerged has been turned around to bring out the best.

A LESSON BORROWED FROM DEVELOPMENTAL PSYCHOLOGY

Any successful program with young children needs to emphasize the incentives and consequences for the child either behaving or not behaving. Raising your voice, scolding, repeating yourself and lecturing kids lets them know what you want, but these actions don't necessarily impact your child. From our experience, these strategies simply don't work very well. You may want them to behave in a certain way, but unfortunately they don't necessarily care about it just because you do.

Did you ever use "reverse psychology" when your kids were little? Did your ever say, "No, no, don't eat your spinach!" to your two-year-old and see them giggle hysterically as they eagerly shoveled it down? This same strategy can work with older kids as well. Kids who are commonly labeled "spirited," "strong-willed" or "stubborn" are ripe for this approach. In fact, playfully telling a child not to do something, or at least giving them a real choice—that's when the magic begins. This is an essential feature of the star chart explained in Chapter 9.

The trap that many parents fall into is caring more about how their child is behaving than the child does. The more that parents push their kids to behave, the more the child pushes back. These efforts usually backfire and create a counter-reaction. This makes sense from the standpoint of developmental psychology because kids in the 3 to 10-year-old age range are naturally differentiating from their parents as they become their own persons. It's part of growing up. The idea of using reverse psychology, particularly with the star chart that we will describe, will be a key element of your success.

TESTING, TESTING 123

Strong-willed kids who are acting out essentially have two different competing "sub-selves" operating. One self is saying "I'm the boss and I want to run the show and do whatever I can get away with. Just do what I want all the time, everything will be fine, thank you very much!"

The other sub-self, that they may be less aware of, feels guilty and bad for getting away with so much. When kids have too much power they become anxious and keep searching to find clearer boundaries. They have more power than they can handle. Therefore, the best way to conceptualize a child's misbehavior and defiance is that the child is testing. Like the old country-western lyrics "Looking for love in all the wrong places," we often quip that these kids are "looking for limits in all the wrong places."

The best way to describe and define your child's strong-willed and out of control behavior is that he or she is testing you. Kids thrive when they are provided with appropriate limits. In fact, they will continue to test, push, shove and prod until you respond appropriately and provide a safe container for their behavior and impulses. The challenge then, is how to provide these boundaries and structure in a way that is not only caring and respectful, but also effective.

CHAPTER FOUR

REDUCING NEGATIVE EMOTIONS

*The uncertainty of parenting can bring up feelings in us that range
from frustration to terror.*
-Brene Brown

$\mathcal{B}$y the time most parents seek psychological help, they have typically tried a number of fairly unsuccessful strategies for getting their children to behave. The common thread is the high level of frustration that happens when a child basically ignores you.

It's normal to have lots of big feelings—fear, anger, hurt—when your child is misbehaving. One of the most upsetting moments is when your kid is "in your face" with defiance, and one of the most common traps parents fall into in these moments is to yell at them.

It can really push your buttons when you feel disrespected and ignored. Funny thing, but your kids don't consider all the ways that you've sacrificed yourself for their benefit. Inside, if you're honest with yourself, you're probably thinking "I break my butt to provide you with your toys and privileges and the life that you have, and here you are, you ungrateful little ****, not listening to me when I'm simply asking you to brush your teeth!" Although very normal, this feeling of outrage can create overwhelming guilt in loving parents.

An essential element of the Win-Win Way is to parent without a lot of emotional upset. The existence of mirror neurons in the brain makes clear the disadvantages of angry parenting.

WHY MIRROR NEURONS MATTER

An important discovery from the world of neuroscience and brain imaging is the existence of mirror neurons, first seen in monkeys and later found in humans. Whenever we are observing someone else, our mirror neurons fire, mimicking in our brains what is going on in the brain of the other person. **Emotions are contagious!** When we see emotions in another's face, we immediately sense that same feeling in ourselves. This discovery helps us to understand why children learn through imitating and how empathy is wired in biologically.

When it comes to families, mirror neurons have important implications. We are constantly impacting and being affected by the mood states of those around us. Haven't you had the experience of feeling perfectly fine, then meeting up with your husband or wife who looks angry or upset only to have them ask why you are upset with them? Now we know that a subtle unconscious dance is going on behind the scenes. Although misery may not love company, misery finds company quickly when the mirror neurons fire. Equally true, if you yawn or get the giggles, you are sure to be joined by people around you.

Because kids reflect our emotional states, our parenting anger gets recycled back into the family in a never-ending downward spiral. Without warning, the hurricane blows in. Negative emotions escalate into mean words and actions we later regret. "NO SCREEN TIME FOR THE REST OF THE WEEK!"

Some kids express their anger immediately and directly. They hit, kick, or say things like "I hate you!" or "You're a terrible mom." Other kids express their anger indirectly or passive-aggressively by taking their sweet time when we need them to get in the car and off to school. Alternatively, their anger can get directed at siblings, peers, a family pet or at school. Sound familiar?

TOOLS TO HANDLE YOUR OWN ANGER

Now that we've established the importance of lowering negative emotions in the family, here are some tools to help you parent more calmly. There are two different methods of handling upsets, each useful in a different way. We recommend that you practice both:

1. Expressing your feelings on your own in a constructive manner.

2. Using methods of deep breathing and centering to calm you down.

EXPRESSING FEELINGS CONSTRUCTIVELY

Expressing feelings in constructive ways helps heal our bodies, relationships, and families. Rather than trying to hold feelings of anger in when your child is pushing all your buttons, it's best to let them out, but not by yelling at your child.

Studies suggest that we heal more rapidly from physical injury and pain when we express ourselves. When people hold feelings inside, they can develop symptoms of depression and low self-esteem. There is also a greater tendency to develop psychosomatic symptoms such as stomachaches, bed-wetting, gastrointestinal problems, rashes, headaches, etc. We want you to learn how to parent more effectively, but not by repressing your feelings.

Perhaps one of the best metaphors for stockpiling feelings is to think about kitchen garbage. If you let a bunch of chicken bones and soup cans sit around too long without taking the garbage out, things start to stink up a bit. The same can be true with feelings. They need to be attended to. You may be fooling yourself if you simply try to ignore the fact that you are really upset with your child. It's okay to be angry. Feelings just are. It's what you do with them that matters.

The first step is to become more aware of what you are feeling moment to moment, and let that be okay. Listen to your body. For example, angry feelings are often stored as tension in the jaw, back, shoulders and/or neck. You can also ask others to give feedback about what they think you might be feeling by how you look. It's usually easier to recognize anger in others than it is for us to own it ourselves.

When we can release some of our anger when we are alone, its power is usually reduced. Sometimes it even goes away. With less charge, our annoyance can then be channeled into constructive conversation. Regular physical exercise also helps reduce anger levels, especially when using the following procedure: Think about an upsetting situation as you exercise aerobically, screaming the words in your head that express what you are feeling and wanting. After that, release the remaining tension with heavy exhalations.

Years ago, a client came up with a brilliant idea that we have recommended ever since. As a child, she had been parented in a harsh manner, constantly yelled at by her mom. When her own children were acting up, her temperature would rise rapidly and she'd naturally want to scream at them. Instead, she would slip into the bathroom, hold a towel up to her mouth (so that no one could hear her) and scream out her frustrations into the towel, often swearing as well. Then she'd take a couple of heavy sighs and then approach the kids to set limits in a respectful, quiet manner, This procedure works wonders to change the anger dynamic that brings out the worst in everybody.

A precautionary note: Although the methods we describe can be useful for people with a history of explosive anger, sometimes more is needed. It is essential to find means of expression that are not hurtful to others. If this is too difficult to accomplish on your own, be sure to seek professional help and guidance.

METHODS OF CALMING

Below are several methods to calm emotions. Ideally you will apply them at the earliest moment you realize you are upset.

- Simply walk away from the situation and give yourself some space.

- Take some long, slow deep breaths. Make sure to fill your lungs up completely and breathe out the tension as you exhale.

- Some people like to close their eyes for a few moments. Splashing your face with water can also have a calming effect.

- If you have the ability to either look out a window or walk outside, try having a brief encounter with nature.

Rather than just focusing on the crisis moments, it also helps to take preventative measures of reducing stress. Practice some form of self-calming at least once or twice daily when you're not on the firing line. People don't think twice about routinely brushing their teeth. If you practice self-relaxation or meditation for five minutes twice a day for the rest of your life, you will be more able to successfully calm your emotions when you need to do so quickly.

USING THE COMBO

We recommend that you experiment with all of the methods described above, seeing what works best for you. In our experience, however, using both of the general strategies works best. For any given circumstance that really upsets you, try expression first and calming methods second—for example, screaming in a pillow and then quieting yourself before interacting with your child. Don't worry that you'll have to be escaping to another room to scream in a towel for the rest of your parenting days. After a few weeks of practice, most parents no longer need to express as much, especially because levels of stress have fallen so dramatically after implementing all of the methods of the Win–Win Way.

AIM FOR DETACHMENT

From the standpoint of human dynamics, one of the most significant problems for families with kids out of control is that the parents care how their child is behaving, but the child cares very little. What can work better for you, paradoxically, is to learn how to operate from a psychological space where you don't care so much. Of course, you care immensely about your child but you need to be less devastated or upset by the acting out behaviors. See them as calls for love and limits. This new insight fosters the detachment you need to parent calmly and effectively. The goal is to help kids want to behave for reasons other than just because you want them to.

With this model, you are simply providing incentives and consequences for behavior so that your child has increased motivation to cooperate. Here are some examples of ways we suggest that you give your child a choice to comply or not.

- ■ "Nathan, would you like to pick up your toys like I asked, or would you rather spend some time in the corner?"

- ■ "Samantha, you can either hand me the iPad right now, or would you like me to take it away for an hour?"

- ■ "Juniper, do you want to stop talking to me like that or shall I take away some time from your TV tonight?

No big drama, no standing over the child, no attachment (as in being attached or driven to get a certain outcome). If you have an investment in things being a certain way, kids will simply rebel. The paradox is that the more you don't care how your child behaves and simply let the consequences work, the more your child will start to care and step up to the plate.

Imagine that a police officer pulls you over for speeding. He doesn't warn you, scold, lecture, guilt trip, hit you or repeat himself. He just gives you a ticket. And if that's not enough to do the trick, the subsequent one costs even more. Although we don't want to play cops and robbers, the use of appropriate consequences prepares our kids for the real world.

CHAPTER FIVE

WHY TO AVOID SPANKING

Power is of two kinds. One is obtained by the fear of punishment and the other by acts of love. Power based on love is a thousand times more effective and permanent then the one derived from fear of punishment.
-Mahatma Gandhi

*O*ne of the goals of this book is to give parents effective tools so that they can stop spanking their young children. The Win-Win Way is not only more effective, it also teaches cooperation, respect and a non-violent way to work out conflicts.

Although a few prominent authors and parenting experts still advocate the use of spanking, most discourage the use of any forms of physical punishment, viewing these as both harmful and unnecessary. Despite this, a high percentage of parents still spank their kids. The primary disadvantages of spanking are the following:

■ It sends the message that a good way to get what you want is to use physical force or violence. Kids who are spanked at home tend to see aggression as a legitimate way to work out differences with others, regardless of any advice we may give as parents. Why? Because they are far more likely to do what we do than to do what we say.

■ Spanking provokes angry feelings that the child may later direct toward peers, siblings, pets—or, more than likely, back at you. Resentment builds up until it is unleashed, often in an altogether different context.

- Hitting your child can damage their self-esteem. Since kids identify so closely with their bodies, spanking leaves them with the impression that <u>they</u> are bad rather than that their behavior is unacceptable. To be happy and healthy, children need to feel good about themselves and know that they are loved even when their behavior is not appropriate.

Considering the harmful side effects, all of which have been widely publicized in the media, why do so many parents still spank their kids? The simplest explanation is that, in the absence of new models, most of us repeat history, especially when we are stressed or triggered. Physical punishment also gives the illusion of being effective because it can abruptly but temporarily stop unwanted behaviors. Trapped in the moment, we become too myopic to see the bigger picture involving the build-up of anger and other long-term side effects.

Another reason why parents continue to spank their children is to vent their own frustrations. Once adults learn how to deal with negative feelings in healthier ways, we can better take care of ourselves, no longer at our children's expense. We describe much more about this important topic in Chapter Two of *How's Your Family Really Doing?* As we have emphasized, expressing feelings in healthy ways is essential to being happy and loving in families.

Parents from all walks of life have begun to make a shift away from spanking. In reshaping their approach to discipline and adding lavish doses of positive attention, these parents have not only corrected problems, but greatly enhanced harmony and good feelings for the whole family. Even some of the most strong-willed kids imaginable have become cooperative and well behaved with this non-violent approach.

CHAPTER SIX

FAMILY RULES

Our children are counting on us to provide two things: consistency and structure. Children need parents who say what they mean, mean what they say, and do what they say they are going to do.
-Barbara Coloroso

$\mathcal{W}$e have seen parents at both extremes of the spectrum—those who are too strict, and those with hardly any clear, consistent rules whatsoever. Outlining basic rules and routines helps kids know what is expected of them and what behaviors are out of line. It makes life run more smoothly and lowers children's anxiety to know what's what.

Some rules may be implied, like respecting others or being kind, and others spelled out very specifically, such as bedtimes or curfews. Some rules exist for small children; others apply to everyone. As with striking a balance between too soft and too firm, healthy families balance the need for clear rules and consequences without creating so many rules that it's hard to keep track.

If you haven't already done so, you may want to sit down with your parenting partner and write down your family rules. The very process of discussing them may lead to some interesting and/or difficult conversations—and surface any potential conflicts that need to be resolved first. Airing these differences before you try to institute this program is a must. When stuck, you may want to talk to other parents who are effective at setting limits and whose kids are under control.

Another issue that can make this approach less effective is when one or both parents do not honor the rules set in the family meeting. One of the most powerful ways parents can teach their kids rules is living by them. There is an old adage that seems to apply well:

What children hear, they mostly forget. What they see, they mostly remember. What they do, they understand and internalize.

Although there are some exceptions, the majority of family rules should apply to everybody. If the rules are supposed to be for everybody, but you break them, you're in effect saying, "Do what I say—not what I do!" Or, "Just wait until you grow up. Then you can break all the rules you want."

For example, if you make a family rule that everybody's room has to be kept presentable but your bedroom remains a mess, you're sending a mixed message. Rest assured that either your child's room will look the same as yours or that rebellion or resentment will soon be on the loose. The same thing goes for your manner of speaking to one another. If you are putting your kids in time out for yelling, and then you and your mate yell at one another in front of them, it will be more confusing and usually far less effective.

WHAT ARE APPROPRIATE RULES?

Rules provide a road map for helping family members get along with each other and with others in the outside world. They fall into several basic categories. First and most crucial are rules that keep children and teens safe. Protection is the reason for teaching small children not to get in cars with strangers and for creating serious consequences when teens drink and drive. If you are trying to change a global pattern of permissiveness, start with basic safety rules and go from there.

The second area for rules has to do with respecting other people's boundaries, which include physical space and touch, sensitivity to needs and feelings, and respect for property and privacy. Some common examples: knocking on the bathroom door, not hitting or name-calling, and asking before borrowing something. Some of these standards of good behavior become long-term projects, requiring intervention in different ways depending on the child's age.

Most families run more efficiently with a clear set of expectations about maintaining a neat and orderly environment. What rules do you have about putting things away, having chores, keeping rooms tidy, noise and activity levels, et cetera? Far too often, we see families where both mom and dad work full-time jobs yet they are still doing all the housework. What message does it send the children about the importance of sharing responsibilities or pitching in to help, or about everyone doing their part? Parents are constantly teaching their children values, whether consciously or not.

Another arena where most families have rules pertains to personal responsibilities. Once children begin school, we generally expect them to attend faithfully, to participate as best they can, and to complete whatever tasks or homework they are given. Most parents tell kids that school is like their "job," and just as mom has to be at work on time and dressed appropriately, they have to go to school having had a good night's sleep and a healthy breakfast.

If you are implementing this program for the first time and were one of those families with few or no explicit rules when you started, go slowly. Start with no more than three of the most serious or difficult behaviors that you want to address first before moving to some of the other areas mentioned above. Examples include hitting, talking back, or open defiance. The first step is to slow down the runaway train. If you try to change too much, it is more likely you will get burned out before the program has the chance to take effect.

"SCREEN TIME" RULES

We have entered a new age of electronics and mass communication unlike any other generation has ever encountered. Ron Taffel, Ph.D., addresses this issue masterfully in *Childhood Unbound: Saving Our Kids' Best Selves—Confident Parenting in a World of Change* (2009). Rather than burying our heads in the sand or lamenting on how the world has gone to hell in a hand basket, Taffel recommends, as do we, that parents find ways to enter into this brave new world with their children.

In the old days, this was not such an issue. Most families had the same rule: you can watch TV or talk on the phone when you're finished with homework. TV shows weren't available 24/7 and very few kids even had phones in their rooms. It's not so simple anymore...

Parents today are wise to have clear rules about cell phones, iPads, games, computers, and TV, establishing guidelines when the children are young. This means deciding how much time per day you want your child to be having screen time and sticking to it. Based upon scores of brain and behavioral studies, the American Academy of Pediatrics recommends not more than one to two hours per day of screen time. We typically recommend an hour and a half.

More than that amount can have negative effects on children's school performance, particularly scores in reading. Research on ten and eleven year olds has found that children allowed more than two hours of daily screen time were sixty-one per cent more likely to have social and emotional problems as well. (Page, et al., 2010).

Young kids can have anxious reactions to images that they've seen on TV and need a bubble of protection from many of the worries of the world—war, Ebola, or even climate change. We've seen eight-year-olds in our practice who've been traumatized by the evening news. To make monitoring easier, we also recommend that kids not have TVs in their bedrooms, but instead locate them in common areas. This keeps them from holing up in their rooms where you can't connect with them, let alone know what they are really up to.

The Internet has opened up both extraordinary amounts of useful information and also the dangers of uncensored, unprotected sites. Children can be damaged by overexposure as well as inappropriate exposure to information, images, and predators on the Internet. In addition to rules about how much daily time is allowed, it is helpful to establish guidelines about what sites are appropriate given the age of your child.

In a recent case, a nine-year-old boy was caught waking up every night in the wee hours to look at porn on his iPod. His parents hadn't been sophisticated enough with technology to realize that this was even possible. They needed help not only with that challenge, but also learning how to work together in setting appropriate boundaries and limits in other ways as well.

Another reminder about how imitative children are: if you want your kids to be doing things other than watching TV, talking on the cell phone, or being on the computer, you may have to start by monitoring and changing your own behavior. Don't keep the TV on at all times or talk or text on the cell phone at dinner. In fact, we recommend electronic free times when the family just hangs out together—such as during mealtimes, family outings, or after a certain time of day.

Many teens have confided in us, sharing their secret of how they text their friends long into the night. They feel anxious with the threat of feeling even momentarily disconnected from their "tribe" of peers. For some kids this pattern is problematic and requires more monitoring and limits. It also works well to empathize with how hard it can be to feel cut off from their friends. Many knowing families have adopted a rule where electronics are checked into kitchen charging stations at night before going to bed.

When it comes to computer and videogames, there is also evidence that certain children and adults have an addictive tendency that makes this form of activity a serious problem. We have seen kids and adults who have flunked out of school, lost jobs, and lost relationships because of their obsession with gaming. Developing healthy habits is easiest done day by day from childhood on.

CHAPTER SEVEN

THE BIG PICTURE

There are only two lasting bequests we can hope to give our children.
One of these is roots, the other, wings.
-Johann Wolfgang von Goethe

*I*n general, people become motivated to act in certain ways through the influence of both internal and external factors. We are either motivated from within, from without, or both. We love our jobs because of the immense satisfaction of helping others and also because we can earn a living, pay the bills and take fun vacations.

Internal incentives usually work the best. Think about activities that you pursue because you love how they make you feel. It could be sports, hiking, arts or crafts, writing, poetry or dancing. You do these things for the pure enjoyment they bring. The same is true with kids. Remember, they naturally want to act in more loving and respectful ways. They feel scared, guilty and bad about themselves when effective limits are lacking.

INCENTIVES AND CONSEQUENCES

The external incentive for kids with the Win-Win approach is an opportunity to receive positive adult attention, love, and spend fun time together. The highly reinforcing internal incentive for kids to behave includes the fact that they feel more secure, in control of themselves and their circumstances, and they are relieved of guilt.

The primary form of negative consequence used with the Win-Win Way is a quick and simple form of time-out that has the side benefit of providing practice in emotional self-regulation—the ability to calm oneself down as big feelings arise. These aspects provide the perfect catalyst for kids to shift to what they want to do anyway—behave better and feel better about themselves as a result.

ESSENTIAL PROCEDURES

- The family meeting that sets up a framework for the whole process

- The 5:1 ratio of positive interactions

- The creation of family rules

- The use of a unique kind of star chart

- A new kind of time-out that becomes the primary form of negative consequence

- A back-up procedure for when a child refuses to accept a time-out

- The playful use of reverse psychology

We find it best to use all of the six elements together, and to implement them all at the same time. Neglecting to use all of the procedures together increases the chance of your being disappointed with the results.

The success of this program is dependent upon how it is introduced and presented to the kids. It's the beginning of a whole new way of being together as a family and can backfire without adequate preparation for the change it will bring about for all of you. How you will introduce this new parenting model and how to conduct a family meeting to introduce it to your child will be described in Chapter 13.

Now that you understand the reasons for this new approach, we will go through the practical procedures, one by one. Once again, we encourage you to read through the whole book before implementing the program.

CHAPTER EIGHT

THE 5:1 RATIO

Everything has beauty, but not everyone sees it.

-Confucius

$\mathcal{T}$he 5:1 ratio means that positive interactions with your child should be happening at least five times as frequently as negative ones. Yes, that's really five positives for every negative. To reinforce children means to praise, thank, smile, hug, or give them something they like. One of the most powerful reinforcements for younger children is adult attention. It's more powerful than any other influence and doesn't cost a cent or create attachment to food or material goods.

The 5:1 ratio is used to increase the number of positive interactions and warmth with your child to protect against the fact that this new approach is such a huge, and sometimes, unsettling change. You are changing the rules on them, and that won't seem fair, particularly at the beginning.

The implementation of this program is like an elective family surgery. When you go into surgery, you are given an IV drip that floods your veins with glucose, antibiotics and vitamins and minerals that are poised to fight off infection and potential problems.

Changing the rules can be very hard on kids, and some dramatic flare-ups are likely to occur until they settle into the new routine.

It's well worth the investment, but just like with surgery, things are likely to get worse before they get better.

The use of reinforcements is the backbone of effective discipline because it relies on positive rather than negative control. Since parents are such powerful models for their kids, it teaches them to be positive as well.

A generally positive approach also reminds your children that they are loved for who they are, which will increase the effectiveness of any occasional punishment you use. The warmth of your connection helps them care more about how you'd like them to behave. Positive actions with each family member add to the bank account of your relationships, whereas negative ones can bankrupt you.

Catch your child doing something good and reinforce it!

THE RIGHT KIND OF PRAISE

The use of praise, although a good thing, can be misdirected or overdone. Some parents have been misguided in their well-meaning attempts to protect their child's self-esteem at all costs. You want to help your children feel special and important, but not send the message that they are the center of the universe. When kids are praised for how wonderful they are, no matter what they are doing, they can become arrogant and develop an entitled, over-inflated sense of themselves. Children are also smart enough to know when parents' endless praise is undeserved or overinflated.

For example, children who are told that they are brilliant can assume that if they are so smart then it's bad to make mistakes. It is best to praise a child's ability to stick to a task rather than to use labels like "intelligent," "great artist," etc. Psychologists and business leaders alike agree on the importance of grit to later success in life. Grit is perseverance in the face of obstacles combined with a passion for long-term goals. Teach the importance of practice and effort instead. Children learn best when provided with constructive criticism as well as praise in the context of a warm and caring relationship.

CHAPTER NINE

THE STAR CHART

The reward for work well done is the opportunity to do more.
-Jonas Salk

*I*n addition to the 5:1 ratio, the star chart provides a great incentive for kids to want to listen and behave better. The chart works because it maximizes children's incentives to do well out of their own self-interest—not just because you want them to, but because they do. A typical chart will last only a few months, and a typical response for kids is that they will show a pretty dramatic turnaround and eventually no longer need the incentive.

It's best to avoid the use of material rewards. The use of things like money and candy can become expensive and also lead to a reliance on bribes and incentives later on. The stars in this chart earn a child special time each evening when they get to be in charge and have their parents give them special, individual, undivided attention.

Star Chart for: _____

Directions: At the end of each day, award a star for effort or improvement on each of the behavior categories

Behavior Goals	Mo	Tu	We	Th	Fr	Sa	Su
	○	○	○	○	○	○	○
	○	○	○	○	○	○	○
	○	○	○	○	○	○	○
	○	○	○	○	○	○	○
	○	○	○	○	○	○	○

If you would prefer to download an 8 ½ by 11" template of our star chart instead of copying the one on the previous page, go to **Strong-WilledChild.com**. It is located under "Forms." Feel free to make as many copies as you'd like.

As you glance across the top of the star chart page, notice that there is one column going down for each day of the week. For the column on the left hand side of the page there is a space for the listing of target behaviors.

The first thing to do in setting up an effective chart is to determine target behaviors that will be the focus for earning stars. Choose three of the most problematic behaviors that your child is struggling with right now. It might include a star for "listening or minding," "not hitting, " or "using your words" instead of acting out on feelings.

A fourth star is assigned for "time out compliance." After you have read and understood the section on time out, you will see the importance of this star. Finally, a fifth star is to be used as a "gimme" star. Figure out a specific behavior where your child is already around 95% compliant. Examples might include brushing their teeth when asked, clearing dishes after a meal, etc.

AWARDING THE STARS

Kids in the three to ten-year-old age range respond best when consequences for behavior, either positive or negative, happen within minutes or hours rather than days. This star chart gives your child feedback each evening about the number of stars they have earned that day. Kids receive an immediate payoff, as yet to be described. (We bet you can't wait.)

Children earn their stars for improvements and effort rather than for achievement. In the beginning it is essential to lower your expectations to the point where, ideally, kids are given three to five

stars each day. It is better t(
the stars rather than withh(
fun of the system, further 1
their behavior.

On the other hand, the s
not be too easy. It's okay to 1
child earns just a couple of
can increase in difficulty o\
make the system achievable 1

34

In our experience, a
their father as part of
some reason, othe
fights, hide-and
kids like to p
certain ro

THE BIG PAY-OFF

The star chart works with kids not only because they feel special for earning the stars, but also because they get to cash them in with you each evening. Approximately an hour before their bedtime, you sit down with them and give them feedback about the day. You want to emphasize the positive things that you've noticed. A common example is "Wow, I noticed this afternoon that you were really frustrated with your little brother, but you caught yourself and used your words instead of hitting him. Great job!"

Your kids will be earning special reward time with you according to the number of stars they have earned for that day. Decide the total amount of time that you can give your kids. Ideally, they would be able to earn 5 minutes per star for a possible 25 minutes per day if they earned all 5 stars. If your schedule only permits 15 minutes total per day, that would imply offering just 3 minutes per star. 20 minutes total time available would equal 4 minutes per possible star.

For whatever amount of time the child has earned, they get to be in charge and "make you do" whatever they choose for that evening. Having earned this precious, fun, special time for their efforts, your child gets their shot at being the one Who's the Boss. (Be sure to use the procedure described in Chapter 13, Step 5, as the way that you inform the kids about the Star Chart.)

out 90% of boys choose wrestling with their reward time. If you can't wrestle for options can work equally well, such as pillow go-seek, flashlight games, or board games. Other ay dress-up with their moms or have parents act out a e in fantasy play.

The essential point is that the child gets to choose the activity and be the boss unless they are asking you to do something that isn't okay by your standards. (Don't do anything dangerous or illegal.) It is also best to avoid activities that include electronics, or just watching TV together, etc. Some kids really like to earn extra story time where they are being read to, and that works fine. The bottom line with the chart is that kids become eager to behave during the day in order to earn this extra special attention time that evening. That's why the situation becomes so beneficial for all involved.

One of our funniest stories involved a straight-laced dad who had slightly misinterpreted our intentions about the star chart. He was thrilled to see the dramatic improvement in his daughter's behavior in the first week, but innocently asked how long he had to keep doing "chicken dances." We found out that his daughter had cashed in on five stars a night by asking him to dance like a chicken around the living room to one of her favorite songs. Although he was more than willing to pay this price for her continued improvement, we reminded him that the payoff for the stars is to share an activity <u>together</u>.

If you happen to be parenting alone, have two kids, or don't have the time in the evening to give each child five minutes per star, the best way to handle this is to discuss the situation with your children and ask them to compromise. See if they can agree upon a special, fun activity you can all do together. If you're going it alone day after day, have your kids alternate between who chooses the activity each day.

An essential element of this system is, on an ongoing basis, to prod the kids playfully by asking them not to earn so many stars.

Do it in the morning. You might whisper to your partner (or under your breath) "I hope Avery doesn't get so many stars today....I am so tired of playing that board game." Or "My muscles are so tired from last night, I hope Jake doesn't get so many stars..."

The kids know that you are playing a game with them with these remarks, and you know it too, but it all comes together to enhance the effectiveness of the system. They will respond anyway. Although aimed at serious change, the tone is light and playful—it's a powerful combination. They will defeat you by behaving better— that's the Win-Win Way.

BANKING STARS

As is often the case, sometimes life gets in the way of following through with the pay-offs every evening. Family plans such as going out to dinner or having a late soccer game may make it inconvenient or impossible to follow through on the star chart cash-in on any given day. Although it shouldn't become a habit, it works fine to bank the stars for a special weekend activity. To honor the stars earned but not cashed in, go for a special hike or to the park. Again, we caution against the use of stars for toys or material things. Kids really crave your undivided attention more than anything else.

CHANGING TARGET BEHVIORS

Children will often improve their performance on a target behavior in a matter of weeks. For example, a child will learn to use their words instead of hitting a sibling when they are upset. Feel free at that point to celebrate your child's gains with some big high fives and retire that star category. Then you can re-assess your situation and add a new star for any other challenging behaviors that weren't included in your first chart. It's also fine to retire a star or two and cut down the number that would be included in your daily system.

HOW LONG ARE STAR CHARTS NEEDED?

The real goal with the star chart is to jump-start new habits of behavior. After a period of weeks or months, some kids lose interest. Others like to continue earning stars simply because it helps them to feel good about themselves, even without the pay-off of special fun time. Figure out what works best in your situation. We rarely see cases where the charts become a long-term dependency. The ultimate goal is to get kids to internalize the system, stretch their own wings and behave in ways that are respectful and compliant.

> When we interview kids about how things are going at home with the star charts and new kind of time out, most kids say that they really love the special time they earn with the stars, and appreciate the short length of time of time outs. One mom came up with the idea of putting herself on a star chart and have her kids playfully give her stars as she worked hard to improve her yelling at them.

CHAPTER TEN

A UNIQUE FORM OF TIME OUT

Kids won't come out and thank you each and every time you make a decision they aren't totally fond of.... But in their hearts kids know you're doing your job, just like they are doing their job by arguing.
-Fred Gosman

*M*any parents have read or have been told to use a system where they time out kids by placing them in their room for one minute per age of the child. That means that an eight year old is supposed to spend eight minutes in their room. It didn't take us long as clinicians to figure out that this common myth didn't make much sense. Here are just a few reasons why:

- Kids can happily play in their room, so it's often not effective as a deterrent.

- Kids can get destructive in their rooms, breaking things, hurting themselves, or even trying to escape out a window.

- Kids are often not sufficiently well-behaved enough to stay in their rooms when told. They will leave the room without being given permission to do so, and then parents have to either lock or hold a door closed.

- Kids are not necessarily learning emotional self-control because the length of their time out isn't dependent on their ability to listen to you, get their act together, and settle down.

THE NEW PROCEDURE

We find that the best kind of time out is for a child to stand facing a corner for a very short period of time. No blame, no shame. For kids who are 3-5 years old, the amount of time that they have to do a time out can be as little as thirty seconds. However, and this is a big however, they have to be quiet in the corner, standing up and not making noise for the thirty seconds in order to fulfill their consequence and be allowed to leave the corner.

If your child wants to sing, talk, or tap their fingers on the wall, that's fine. They can wiggle around and sing the "Star-Spangled Banner" for hours if they would like, just as long as they stay there. But their thirty-second time period only starts and is completed by complying with the rules. On the other hand, they don't have to stand at attention like a little foot soldier.

The goal is that when kids are asked to do a time out, they should respond accordingly. You should not have to walk or guide them over to the corner. Even more important, you shouldn't drag them over or hold them there. The obvious goal is for the child to obey when being sent to a time out, experience the consequence, and then be given permission by the parent to come out and celebrate. Yes, celebrate! High fives and hugs are in order because they have been able to accomplish this.

THE TIME OUT STAR

Kids usually want to finish a time out quickly and successfully because it's not all that fun to stand in the corner. They are also earning a star for compliance in time out. These incentives help kids learn to accept consequences for their behavior, and also to settle themselves down more quickly.

The time out star that kids earn on their star charts has to do with the following criteria:

1. Kids earn the star when they have shown improvement in their ability to readily accept a time out and go to the corner when asked.

2. They can also earn this star by being able to spend less time finishing a time out successfully. For example, their time in the corner is closer and closer to that thirty-second time period.

3. A third criterion for earning the time out star is that a child needs fewer or no time outs in the course of any given day.

TEACHING THE NEW PROCEDURE

The best way to teach kids about the new form of time out is to role-play it in the family meeting (as described in Chapter 13). Pretend that you are the child, say or do something that might get them a time out, and then go to the corner and kick the wall, dramatically asking "Can I come out now?" Let the kids giggle as they see you struggle with trying to do it right, then finally get it straight. Share with the kids that there's a really important secret about how they can learn to finish a time out more quickly and get some fun stars for improvement—whisper the hint about how it helps if you take a few slow deep breaths.

> A demonstration of this procedure can be found at **Strong-WilledChild.com**. Click on Video Demos where it says "Time Out."

Developing the ability to have emotional self-control in the face of adversity is a huge, beneficial side effect of this kind of corner time. As kids learn how to manage difficult feelings in time out, they gain mastery over other impulses. This newly acquired skill tends to generalize to other behaviors as well. One child bragged,

"My brother just knocked over my Lego tower but now I know how to keep out of trouble and not hit him!"

The goal of time out is to give kids greater control over their behavior and emotions—similar (hopefully) to how adults manage frustrations. There is no shame involved in this process, and we don't advocate timing kids out in front of their friends. Using this procedure provides practice in exercising self-control in the face of upset. This is a skill that they need and will benefit from for the rest of their lives.

ADDITIONAL GUIDELINES

- Establish a few different time out spots in your house. If you don't have any corners in your house that are free from things to play with, such as a bookcase or even window shades, select a blank wall instead. One good spot is in the living room so that you can see what your child is doing without having to interrupt your activities. An exception to this is when there's a TV or other distractions happening.

- Because you are giving your child practice at managing emotions, it's best not to hover to keep them in the corner. Occupy yourself with an activity in the next room, allowing them to save face, glancing over occasionally to see if they have settled down and are ready to start their compliance.

- If you have more than one child, ask your other children to leave the room when doing a time out. Brothers and sisters can sometimes add fuel to the fire of the child in the corner by laughing, teasing or taunting their sibling.

- If a time out is needed out-of-doors, have them face a telephone pole or tree. If you are in a store and your child needs a time out, take them outside and have them face an outside wall of the store, preferably around a corner. In all cases in public, make sure to minimize public display, shame and embarrassment.

AN ALTERNATIVE TO TIME OUT

Although we advocate the use of time out as the go-to tool for most misbehavior, it's also fine to use consequences related to a child's acting out. For example, a solution for the abuse of a toy is to withdraw the privilege of the use of that toy for an hour or so, depending on the age of your child.

Kids today often ignore their parents when asked to stop playing an electronic game. Simply take away screen-time privileges for a while. Remember, however, that consequences are like medicine. Using too little can be ineffective, while using too much can increase resentment. Recommended times can range from the loss of an hour to the rest of the day. Start with a shorter amount of time, building up only as needed. With young children it's best to start each day with a clean slate and all privileges returned.

CHAPTER ELEVEN

THE BACK-UP TO TIME OUT

Believe me, my children have more stamina than a power station.

-Robbie Coltrane

*I*f your child is inclined to take time outs willingly, consider yourself lucky. You won't need to have a back-up procedure. On the other hand, don't assume that your family situation is tragically hopeless because you can't even imagine that your child will actually obey you and walk to the corner or stay there without being held. This is not unusual and there's a solution.

If your child either leaves the corner before you have given him permission to do so, or if your child doesn't go to the corner when you ask, then the back up procedure for most 3 to 10-year-old kids is to "hold" them on the floor, near the corner.

THE HOLDING PROCEDURE

The holding procedure should also be role-played in a family meeting prior to being used with a child. Once again, you are changing the rules and want to give prior notice. This can often be the most upsetting aspect of the Win-Win approach. However, to the degree that children are so out of control that they won't listen to you and remain in the corner when asked to do a time-out, it is necessary to hold or restrain them until they are ready to do as you have asked.

This procedure takes place with you sitting on the floor, placing your child facing away from you, holding their arms by crossing yours over theirs, and holding their legs by draping your legs over theirs. Depending on the size and strength of the child, it may be safer and more comfortable for you to sit on the floor with your back braced against a wall or sofa. Think of yourself as a big mama or papa bear giving your cub a firm, loving embrace, keeping him safe from the world and himself.

A demonstration of this procedure can be found at
Strong-WilledChild.com. Click on Video Demos
where it says "Holding."

Don't be surprised if your child screams, tries to bite, kick you, wriggle away and calls you every name in the book. Your job is to breathe deeply and, every few minutes or so, reiterate that you will "let them" go stand in the corner when they have gained enough control to do so. Maintain a non-attached, calm attitude. Act as if you have all the time in the world to wait for them to scream and kick while you hold them. (If you have neighbors close by, you may want to warn them about the possible increase in noise.)

A very important element is to keep slow deep breathing while your child is being held. This helps them to quiet down more quickly. You might say something like, "Sweetheart, when you are ready to settle down and listen to mommy and go do your time out, I will let you go. I'm so sorry that this is hard for you because we have changed the rules."

This apology about changing things is crucial in helping your child feel understood about their struggle and adaptation. Your empathy helps them to more quickly make a shift.

During their first holding experience, it is typical for kids to cry, thrash about and protest your newly claimed authority for a number of minutes. The average amount of time can be 10-15 minutes for a first time, and then just a few minutes for subsequent holdings. In our experience, some of the longest times for being held the first time are around 30 minutes. A few headstrong kids fight even loner if they are testing your perseverance. It's usually not as long as you might think.

It is also common to have a second or third time when your child needs to be held, but the time it takes for them to settle down and realize you mean business is shorter than the first. Your child is testing you to make sure that the rules are still in place. Consistency is crucial or you will prolong the entire change process.

After settling down, let them go do their corner time. Then, and only then, is it time for high fives, hugs, and a celebration of their accomplishment. Don't forget this part even though you may be a bit exhausted.

HOW AND WHY HOLDING WORKS

This holding procedure helps in a variety of ways:

1. At a very symbolic level, you are providing an important container and boundary for your child's behavior. To the degree that they are out of control, you are providing the external limits or controls being begged for. Remember that it's very scary for kids to have so much power that they don't listen to you and ignore your requests.

2. Holding your child when he is out of control also provides him with a safe and contained way to express his upset feelings and to release them. The part of your child that still wants to be the boss is having its last hurrah. This catharsis helps kids to shift as well as to mourn the loss of so much power. As they let go of their feelings they are also letting go of their former habits and expectations. They feel both sad and mad that the rules have changed, and as they release the feelings, they become more accepting of the new rules.

3. A third reason for the holding procedure is that it is obviously a back-up consequence or punishment. Although kids don't like it, it's also a safe and minimally punitive way to re-establish control. You are not leaving marks on your child or hurting them in any way. Just hold your child as tightly as needed so that no one is getting injured.

A couple came in with concerns about their seven-year-old son. He'd been adopted at age four and had experienced a pretty rocky first few years of life, living with many different foster families. The parents felt that his early experience made it essential to help him heal his early attachment issues. This appeared to be the case in the first weeks of trying the program. He would refuse to go to time out and had to be held on the floor eight times in ten days. After that, though, he got with the program and improved dramatically.

Then, ironically, a slightly younger (also adopted) daughter took her turn and became temporarily more out of control! After keeping it together for a long time while a brother or sister is acting out, it's not uncommon for a sibling to take a turn at being the one who gets to fall apart—especially when it becomes clear that the parents will contain their pent-up feelings.

EXCEPTIONS TO USING THE HOLDING PROCEDURE

The holding procedure may not be necessary or appropriate for certain kids or situations. As an example, a woman who is pregnant or has back problems may not want to sit on the floor and restrain a child who doesn't want to do a time out. For kids who are as physically strong as their parents, or who are ten years old or older, you may have to figure out another back-up plan.

Failing to accept a time out when asked should be considered a "felony," with a firm and consistent response. Depending on the child and their particular attachments and preferences, we recommend any of the following: taking away a half hour of electronics or screen time, early bedtime, no dessert, removal of a privilege, etc. For kids ages three to ten, it's always best to return full privileges by the next day. Every day is a new day with a clean slate.

CHAPTER TWELVE

TIMING THE TRANSITION

The right thing at the wrong time is the wrong thing.

-Joshua Harris

*I*f you are like most parents, the changes in your parenting style that you are about to bring about are no small matter. Remember in Chapter 8 when we introduced the 5:1 positive to negative ratio and how and why it is a necessary part of this program? We gave the analogy of the preparation done before going in for surgery. Let's go back to that analogy since introducing this program constitutes a dramatic shift in family dynamics.

When you have surgery, things like pain levels often get worse before they get better. That will almost certainly happen with this program, and usually within the first couple of days. You need to brace yourself for an initial reaction of testing by your child.

If you were getting knee surgery, you would go into it knowing that the surgical procedure will hurt and actually temporarily make things worse, but that after a reasonable period of recovery time, your knee will get better. You have to believe that the procedure is necessary, and that it will be both effective and worth your investment.

This process is also like surgery in the sense that you want to be very careful and deliberate in its execution, making sure that you are starting the new program when the timing is right. You won't want to have surgery or do this big transition when:

- You or the kids are sick
- Aunt Theresa is in town
- You have a fun trip planned
- Your schedule requires you to be out of the house for significant periods of time

If more than one parent is involved, it is best that you are both home for the big transition, with all hands on deck for at least a day or two. Having both parents and primary caretakers all involved reinforces the idea that all of the adults are in agreement. This is a big change, and although you should see some positive benefits pretty quickly, there will almost certainly be some rough times in the first few days or week. Remembering that things will probably get worse before they get better will help you stay with the program.

CHAPTER THIRTEEN

THE FAMILY MEETING SET-UP

Alone we can do so little; together we can do so much.
-Helen Keller

*I*magine that you are driving home late one night. Suddenly you see that dreaded flashing light in your rear view mirror, but you are sure you weren't speeding. Unfortunately, the nice highway patrol officer says he clocked you going 75 mph. The speed limit on that road had been lowered to 60 mph but there weren't any signs or notification. Not very fair, huh?

Bear in mind that many of the changes that you will be making may feel similarly unfair to your kids. You're changing the speed limit so it's only fair to give advanced warning about the new rules. If they've been getting away with a cruising speed of 75 mph—a speed that is dangerous to themselves and others, they are at least used to it. Now you will be posting the new speed and set of rules, and letting them know that the new limit is a mere 60.

There is a very specific way that we want you to present this new idea to your kids—in a family meeting. Like a band playing a new gig, you want to have your act together before you take it on the road. You may want to take notes on this section and rehearse it in your head, if not out loud before the big day.

This set-up is a way to think about what's coming down, both for you and the kids. It is the bigger context that frames how things have been, as well as how they will change and why. We would strongly recommend not proceeding at all with this program unless you include this component. It's that important!

Make a plan to sit down with the kids for your family meeting just prior to when you will make the shift. Typically, this might be on a Saturday morning so that you have the weekend to weather the storm of any new reactions. If there are two parents involved, both parents should be included in the explanations. As a rule of thumb, if anyone else like a grandparent or nanny is involved in parenting your kids, let's say, at least fifteen percent of total parenting time, ideally then you would include them in this meeting and the program as well.

Keep reminding yourself that the eventual result of providing more structure and rules is that your children will be happier and healthier. If you approach the changes with some enthusiasm and humor, you will also likely get less resistance. They may initially make a stink about the new regime, but remember that everyone benefits when limits are set in a caring fashion. It's a win-win!

Here's the step-by-step process to explain your intentions to your children in the family meeting:

1. EXPLAIN HOW EVERYONE IS IN THE SAME BOAT

First help the kids understand how connected we are in families. If the kids are young enough to appreciate this concrete experience, have family members sit on the floor and surround themselves with pillows, mimicking what it would be like if you were all floating down a river together in a raft. Have everyone pretend that they are paddling.

Ask what would happen if certain people had to paddle but others didn't pull their weight. Then ask what would happen if one person decided to poke a hole in the boat. Who would sink? The answer, of course is "everybody." The punch line that you obviously want the kids to realize is that, in families we're all in the same boat, and we either sink or swim together.

If you feel like your kids are too old to appreciate this experience, just explain the concept in a way that's fitting for them. Some older kids are fascinated by age-appropriate explanations about mirror neurons and how emotions are contagious.

2. SET NEW GOALS FOR THE FAMILY

The next topic for discussion is the setting of new goals and directions for the family. Tell the kids how you would like things to be—with family members all pitching in to bring out the best in each other. Apologize for whatever mistakes you feel you've made. Express what has been hard for you and what you would like to change about your own actions or reactions towards them. Here are some examples of apologies from parents:

- "I'm really sorry about some of those times when I've lost my temper and have yelled at you. I want to find other ways to help you."

- "I'm sorry that I have made fun of you when you were whining and crying. I want all of us to be happier in our family."

- "I really don't like being mad at you and raising my voice and having to repeat myself so much. I would like us to all get along better."

- "I'm sorry that Dad and I were not on the same page, and we didn't follow through enough on rules. We are going to be on the same team from now on."

Now encourage the kids to share how they would like things to change in the family. Ask what contribution they would like to make. What can they take responsibility for changing? Encourage them to give you feedback about how you can be better parents.

This whole process sets a tone of humility and underscores the notion that we are all human and make mistakes. It also takes the kids off the hot seat to know that the adults have things to learn too. No one is singled out for blame and everyone plays a part in helping the family work better.

3. EXPLAIN HOW PARENTS AND KIDS HAVE DIFFERENT JOBS AND RULES

This next step in your family discussion helps challenge an illusion that is predominant with kids in this age range. They believe that <u>they</u> have rules and things that they have to do but that their parents don't—like going to school, having to go to bed when asked, etc. Here's how this discussion can go:

"In families and life, we all have a job to do. I go to work and my job is to show up, be responsible, do the best I can, and be nice to people. If I don't go to work and decide to hang out in the park instead, I don't get paid. I have to follow rules by paying bills and taxes, stopping at red lights, wearing my seat belt and getting along with neighbors. One of my jobs here at home is to take care of you and help you to learn new things."

"Your job as kids is to have fun, learn new things, do your best at school, and be kind and respectful to others—including family members. Your job is also to listen to us as your parents. You have all kinds of things that we give you (meals, clothes, a bed, trips, toys, electronics) just like we get paid at work. We want things to be the same with you as they are with us. When you follow rules and do your job, there will be lots of positive feedback. When you don't, there will also be some new consequences—like when you are not being respectful, helpful, kind, or following rules."

If your kids are on the younger side, your explanation should be much shorter and simpler. It really helps to honor the kids' feelings about the transition coming up. At least once a day for the next couple of weeks, empathize and apologize about how hard it might be for them to have the rules change.

4. CREATE NEW FAMILY RULES TOGETHER

Now it's time to brainstorm with the kids about the kinds of things that can help everyone get along better in your family. When you brainstorm, you want to generate lots of ideas without evaluating them. Many parents are surprised to realize that their children have had quite similar discussions in their classrooms at the beginning of each school year. As much as they can participate in a respectful and helpful manner, include the kids in your deliberations about new rules and consequences. Write each idea down as the kids spout them off, and offer up any that are missing. In order to prepare for this meeting, sit down with the other parent or parent figure and create a list of the rules that you plan to start with.

It's okay if your kids don't want to be involved or offer constructive solutions. If that's the case, proceed without them. Remember that even the hint of more rules could inspire a revolt. If that's the case just go ahead with the next step. Don't get angry at their lack of involvement or negative vibes, just explain that you would love their input but are happy to set the rules without them if they prefer.

5. THE STAR CHART AND BIG "TADA" ADD HUMOR AND SURPRISE

The next part of your family meeting is the explanation of the win-win system to the kids. If there are two or more parental figures involved, you will begin to whisper to each other, back and forth for a couple of minutes.

"We read that book and it had lots of good things to say, but do you really think we should tell the kids about the next part?"

"I don't know, the authors said it was kind of important, but then..."

"Yeah, I know why you're worried. I am too. The book said that our kids were going to love it, but it might be really hard on us!"

"Well, should we tell them?"

"Gosh, I don't know if we'll be able to do it! Maybe it really will be too hard on us, but it'll make them really happy."

(With this banter of whispers, kids usually are jumping into your laps wanting to know what's up with this thing.)

Once you have enticed the kids, explain how the star charts are going to work and discuss all of the elements we have outlined in Chapter 9. This is the time to show them the charts, and with their input, fine-tune any of the behavioral goals.

The kids will be delighted to hear that they will get to be the boss of you when they earn stars for more positive behaviors. At the same time, inform them that you are the "judge and jury" with the awarding of the stars—in other words that there won't be any arguing about whether they have earned them or not.

6. ROLE-PLAY THE NEW KIND OF TIMEOUT AND BACK-UP

Demonstrations of these procedures can be found at **Strong-WilledChild.com**. Click on Video Demos where it says "Time Out" and "Holding."

In these final elements of the family meeting, explain how you will be using a new form of time out in the corner instead of the old means of responding. Share how you will be helping them learn to be more kind, loving or respectful without you yelling, spanking or sending them to their rooms (or whatever was your former method).

Just as the other parts of the meeting were meant to be both fun and engaging, this can often be the best part. Pretend to be your child and do a number of things in the corner that wouldn't qualify as a time out. Most kids love to see mom or dad pretending to fuss, have a temper tantrum or kick the wall.

Then model the correct way. Ask them to tell you when you are being quiet like you are supposed to be when in time out. Then have each of the kids practice what a good time out looks like, celebrating with high fives and hugs.

> Frank and Kasey had two children ages eight and four. When Frank demonstrated the time out procedure during their family meeting, the kids went into hysterics when their four-year-old daughter begged to practice it and wiggled around dancing in the corner. She didn't even need any time outs for the first couple of weeks, but then later averaged only a couple of time outs a week for the first month.

Finally, it's time to describe and role-play the holding procedure (as seen in the Video Demo). Sit with your child on the floor and do the holding procedure to show them what will happen if they refuse to do a time out. This first time, before any power struggles, let it be a fun experience. The new program is now ready for action.

CHAPTER FOURTEEN

ROADBLOCKS TO CHANGE

*The reason people blame things on previous generations is
that there's only one other choice.*
-Doug Larson

*S*ome parents have difficulty carrying out or following through
with aspects of our approach. This is understandable. It's easy for
us to prescribe these methods of handling things, but they are not
always easy to enact.

The most common roadblock to change for parents is the way
that they were parented as children. If you were one of the lucky
people to have been raised in a happy loving family, you've probably
emerged with many skills and strengths from your past. However,
since most families, even relatively healthy ones, have some bad
habits or downright negative patterns, then these too become part
of one's legacy.

Our histories pack a powerful punch when we've buried
old feelings as a way of avoiding the pain associated with them.
Unfortunately the "unfinished business" from our childhood and
previous relationships also tends to get projected onto and played
out with our partner and/or children. It is sad but true that the
people we love the most in the world become victims of this process.

Have you ever noticed how you can be a successful mature adult but step into your parent's house and instantly feel like a ten-year-old? Or that a certain movie scene has you suddenly in tears? Or that your father can still scowl at you and make you feel ashamed for existing? Chances are that some part of your past has been evoked in the present moment. And it isn't always pretty...

THE PAST IS IMPOSED ON THE PRESENT

Our "emotional brains" allowed us to survive as a species, reacting in a split second to protect us from harm. Instantly, we fight, run or freeze. In survival mode we don't have time to consciously decide when to approach or avoid certain circumstances. Memories of highly intense past experiences get wired into our brains without our awareness. Present day events that remind us of these emotionally charged experiences from the past can trigger the same feelings associated with that experience.

The emotional mind reacts to the present as if the past event were happening again. Furthermore, when we are having strong feelings, the emotional brain can enlist the rational mind to justify that our reactions are being created by the present moment, not realizing the influence of the past memory.

These findings from recent brain research have important implications for how we function. All of us have what we call "buttons" or "triggers" that activate old feelings when we're faced with current circumstances, sights, sounds or smells. Or, as we think about the past, emotional memories may surface and provoke discomfort. Although the experience can be unpleasant, we therapists see this as a good thing. Increased self-awareness helps free us from being slaves of our past.

We playfully challenge clients in therapy, telling them that when they "graduate," one of their final exam questions will be to identify and describe their buttons. We say, "What unfinished issues, unreasonable expectations, or feelings from your childhood or previous relationships are most likely to leak out and affect your efforts to be a good parent?"

Like items left behind and collecting dust in our office lost and found, here are some examples you can sort through. Can you claim any of them?

- "Trying to be positive with my kids is really hard because it makes me mad that I didn't receive encouragement as a kid."

- "I wonder if my chronic anxiety and fears got passed down from the fact that my grandparents just barely escaped from the Holocaust."

- "When my four-year-old daughter says 'No' and gets in my face, it stimulates my anger at my dad for spanking me so much."

- "Doc, do you really think I need to be 'right' all the time because that's what my mom did to me?"

If these examples don't grab you, that's okay but it doesn't let you off the hook. Everyone is different, but we all have buttons that can be pushed, particularly when stressed, tired, or hungry. Hopefully you are now curious to uncover whatever past issues may still be bothering you. Or as threatening as it might feel, perhaps you have the courage to ask your partner or children what they think are your biggest triggers.

Often our buttons are connected to certain expectations, conscious or not, of our children, which are not necessarily realistic. Some parents struggle when their kids' goals, values, and preferences are very different from their own. For example, a very athletic parent may expect their children to love sports more than reading.

Without other frames of reference, we grow up assuming that other families are just like our own. One client said, "Do you mean that not all dads go hide out in the garage every time they feel upset or angry?" Another confessed that he thought that it was normal for people to be in conflict all the time. That was his picture of how things were, and therefore how they should be. Other clients make complaints like, "Despite my decision to never be like my mom, here I am yelling at my kids just like what happened to me!" Still others struggle with the disparity between how their parents treated them as children and how their partner treats them. It is common for men who were spoiled by their moms to expect the same kind of royal treatment from their wives. You can imagine how well this works.

> Brothers and sisters are also important influences. One client spent years with a previous therapist focusing on her parents and the neglect and anger she felt from being ignored and mistreated. She remained stuck. Very little attention had been paid to the fact that her sister had terrorized her and treated her with contempt. She discovered in therapy that she had also unwittingly "created" a number of friendships throughout her life that mimicked her relationship with her sister. She was all too comfortable in the role of being mistreated. It is uncanny how these ghosts of the past chase us around until we turn around and face them.

FAMILY OF ORIGIN ASSESSMENT

If you would like more insight about how your childhood has impacted your current struggles as a parent, you may now want to take the Family of Origin Assessment. This tool can help you to learn how your current family patterns may have been affected by the past. You can find it by turning to Appendix B. If you would prefer to download free 8 ½ x 11 in. copies of it, go to StrongWilledChild.com under the "Forms" tab.

PARENTS WORKING AS A TEAM—OR NOT

Another frequent roadblock to change involves the parent's relationship. In order for this program to unfold successfully, parents must be good leaders. They should carry both the responsibility and the authority to effectively carry out the tasks of family life. When there is more than one parenting figure in the home, it is essential that the adults work together as partners, like co-captains of a team.

Problems can arise if one parent becomes stuck in the role of "bad guy" while the other takes on the role of "nice guy." Like a seesaw, one parent is progressively more permissive as the other becomes more strict, often to compensate for the other's behavior or values. Although attempting to balance each other, they are actually casting one another as the enemy, blaming their partner for the children's problems. Before long, kids begin playing one against the other, and if the parents are unable to work out their differences, conflict intensifies and everyone suffers.

Rebecca and Sam agreed that they wanted their eight and ten-year-old boys to stop the bickering, name-calling and physical battles that troubled everyone. The couple hadn't realized that they were working at cross-purposes when they entered family therapy. In one session, Sam asked the eight-year-old to sit in his chair and listen but then Rebecca inserted, "He can listen and play at the same time." Their son didn't move a muscle. Dad's voice got louder. "Sit in that chair now." It was only when mom agreed with dad out loud that Billy moved to his chair. The couple realized that the kids had been responding to the tiny, subtle ways that their parents weren't being a team.

Rather than putting blame or fault on the other parent, the best solution is for parents to compromise a bit, shifting their weight toward the center of the seesaw. The strict parent needs to bring more love and warmth into their relationship with the children, while the permissive parent must learn to provide structure and set firmer limits. This is the kind of compromised position that this program fosters. In addition, both parents need to agree on basic family rules and expectations. When surrounded by a positive family atmosphere with reasonable, age-appropriate rules and consequences, children naturally learn proper behavior.

Sometimes, even though both parents have agreed to try the Win-Win way, one parent secretly believes that this move is totally unnecessary, typically blaming their mate for being too uptight about the kids' misbehavior. When this happens, the reluctant parent can easily sabotage the whole process by not participating in the family meeting, using time out and/or the star chart.

CHAPTER FIFTEEN

SLEEP AND EXERCISE

Good habits formed at youth make all the difference.
-Aristotle

SLEEP

*W*henever we have our initial session with parents of young children who are no longer napping, we ask a very important question. Do you have to wake your kids up in the morning or are they waking up by themselves?

Parents who have difficulty setting limits with their kids also commonly let them stay up too late or have irregular bedtimes. Recent studies (Colten and Altevogt, 2006) estimate that 50 to 70 million Americans are chronically sleep deprived. The long-term effects of sleep loss have been associated with numerous health risks including hypertension, diabetes, obesity, depression, heart attack, and stroke. These statistics are worse than even a few years ago.

Children (roughly aged five to twelve) who are no longer napping but haven't yet reached puberty are particularly vulnerable to sleep deprivation. This is because they can't sleep in like teens and adults. Teenagers, for example, have the ability to stay up until midnight during weekdays and sleep until two in the afternoon on the weekends. But younger children can't do this. We have never found an exception. A young child who has stayed up until midnight is rarely capable of sleeping past eight in the morning.

Pediatricians are a frequent source of referrals for our clinic. They send us young kids demonstrating emotional outbursts, acts of aggression, irritability, and/or attention deficit challenges. How does this relate to sleep? We now know that the most important time when we replenish serotonin in our brains is during sleep. This neurotransmitter is essential to learning, staying calm, and feeling good, and is produced almost exclusively during REM sleep, while we are dreaming. Not enough sleep and you've got an irritable child subject to meltdown.

The diagnosis and the cure are both simple. If you have to wake young children up in the morning, they aren't getting enough sleep! Try putting them to bed fifteen minutes earlier for a few days, and see if they wake up by themselves. If they still aren't waking up by themselves by the time they need to be up, shift their bedtime earlier by another fifteen minutes until they wake up at the appropriate time each morning.. You might be surprised how many problems either disappear or become controllable by adjusting this one daily routine.

Lester and Tracey showed up for their first session exhausted and frustrated with their nine-year-old son and six-year-old daughter. Both of the kids were doing fine in school but were somewhat strong-willed and out of control at home. They often wouldn't respond to even the most benign requests. Out of pity for their kids because they both worked, their parents let them stay up too late at night. Not recognizing developmental differences, they also let the two kids have the same bedtime. After only a week of implementing new bedtimes, the parents estimated that the kids had improved significantly. They went on to implement the procedures in this book with little resistance from their more rested children.

EXERCISE

According to the Center for Disease Control only 3.8% of elementary schools, 7.9% of middle schools and 2.1% of high schools currently provide daily physical education or its equivalent for the entire school year. Twenty-two percent of schools do not require students to take any physical education at all, despite the fact that research has demonstrated the benefits of regular aerobic exercise. Not only does exercise help our hearts, lungs and our ability to keep weight in check, it helps to reduce tension and stress by boosting endorphins. It has also been shown to lower anxiety and alleviate depression.

Now we know that regular exercise is also helpful to our brains. John Ratey, M.D., author of *Spark: The Revolutionary New Science of Medicine and the Brain* (2008) has compiled research from hundreds of studies that link physical activity to adaptability and resilience.

For most of the twentieth century scientists assumed that people were born with all of the neurons (brain cells) that we would ever get, and that our brains were fully hardwired by adolescence. In 1998 we learned that we actually grow new neurons throughout life, a process called neurogenesis. Exercise is one of the most effective ways of increasing the number of new neurons. Studies have shown that rats allowed to exercise produce at least three times as many new brain cells as non-exercising rats (Ratey, 2008). The same is true for people of all ages.

Through the release of certain proteins, exercise contributes to learning skills and heightens our senses. It improves motivation, confidence and even our tendency to establish and maintain social connections. It also improves our ability to be kind to each other because it strengthens the connections in the prefrontal cortex that calm the amygdala (and therefore our emotional outbursts).

Schools where aerobic exercise has been integrated into the curriculum have shown dramatic decreases in acts of aggression. Test scores go up. It helps both kids and adults focus and maintain attention, even those challenged with Attention Deficit Disorder

(ADD or ADHD). Exercise has also been shown to block addictive cravings of all sorts.

If exercise were a medication, given that it is free, people would be lined up for blocks to get some. Unfortunately, because it takes time and commitment in a world where families are massively overcommitted, this simple solution to many ills is often left by the wayside. Given that schools haven't quite gotten their act together on the exercise front, what better way to spend time together as a family than to get outside and move around a lot!

CHAPTER SIXTEEN

NOT ALL FAMILIES ARE ALIKE

Share our similarities, celebrate our differences.
-M. Scott Peck

DIVORCE AND SEPARATION

*I*n Chapter 12, we recommended carefully choosing the most appropriate time to institute this new program. Depending upon how traumatic your situation has been to your child, it may not make sense to start it when the family is in the middle of a divorce or separation. An important reason that your child might be acting out is because of all the turmoil. Your child's behavioral challenges or meltdowns may be less due to a need for limits and more a need for reassurance in the face of impending loss and change. This kind of temporary crisis can be weathered with extra patience and time spent together until things settle down.

When couples are experiencing a lot of conflict in the divorcing process, children can obviously become victims of the tensions. Many children regress at these times and exhibit behaviors that are atypical. Some single parents struggle with setting limits because they feel sorry that their child has an absent parent. Relaxing the rules a little can be helpful in the short run when your child is experiencing big losses, changes or is sick. Just make sure to restore appropriate rules and limits shortly thereafter to prevent long-term problems.

CO-PARENTING WITH YOUR EX

A crucial difference between a "good" and "bad" divorce from the standpoint of children is the adults' willingness to work together as co-parents. The overriding message is that if there are two houses and four co-captains, the adults must pull together in cooperation. The effort is well worth the energy it takes for the sake of the children.

Work together as a team with your ex-partner to create common guidelines for the big rules, acknowledging that every household has its own idiosyncrasies. For example, insist on agreements about school attendance, bedtime policies, rules for respect, and similar consequences for misbehaviors. Less important are variations between houses on policies or routines around things like snacks, mealtimes, and chores.

When you have your big family meeting with the kids, openly address the issue of the two households. It can be a simple explanation like "You know how sometimes the rules are different at mom's house and dad's house? Well, we are going to use star charts and time out here at our house. I've told your dad about it, and he understands." It often happens that an ex will see the positive changes in the kids and will eventually want to adopt the new system.

Clearly, shifting to the procedures we've described works best if both households and all parenting figures are included and agree on the approach. Sometimes getting that agreement is just not possible, however. If you are divorced, and you are ready to implement this program in your household but the other parent is unwilling, at least give your ex a copy of this book and explain when and why you are going to use the program. You also may want to warn them about the likelihood of the kids being upset for a while before they settle into the new system.

SETTING LIMITS IN STEPFAMILIES

When two families come together, or blend into a stepfamily, a new adult relationship has been formed, leading to additional complications about who's in charge. For example, many stepchildren spend part of the week with dad and his new wife; part of the week with mom and her new partner; part of the week with grandparent caretakers; and several hours a week with a babysitter. Children exposed to so many different arrangements often get confused about the rules, and all the more so if the adults have problems communicating with one another.

Stepfamilies also give rise to divide and conquer tactics. It's amazing how creative kids can be with power plays when mom and dad live in two different places. We have witnessed many different ways that kids act out under these circumstances, even though they may not be conscious of what they are doing.

Favorite strategies include threatening to run away to the other parent's home, divulging partial truths about the other parent's rules, making them seem overly strict or inappropriate, and sweet-talking one parent into greater leniency because of the other's alleged meanness. It comes as no surprise that difficulty with a new partner's children is the number one reason many second marriages end in divorce. Setting appropriate limits is a critical dimension of success.

With regard to your new family, don't expect your children and new partner to like or respect each other too quickly. **The non-biological parent can focus on building the relationship through the elements of praise and the star chart. The biological parent should be the disciplinarian when it comes to rules and consequences.** They should also be the one doing any necessary holding on the floor, as well as the vast majority of time outs. Children accept limits far better from someone with whom they have a loving, long-term bond, and you don't want to taint a new partner with the upset feelings kids can have about this "stranger" telling them what to do.

Finally, reach out for information and support. Going through big transitions is stressful for everyone involved. Excellent books about co-parenting, helping kids through divorce and building stepfamilies can be found in the Self-help Resources section of our website. Also check out local stepfamily support groups and parenting classes in your area. It's best not to go it alone.

SETTING LIMITS IN SINGLE PARENT FAMILIES

Single parents, often criticized in the media in recent years, are perfectly capable of being in charge and setting effective limits. In fact, many single parents are far more successful at it after separating from a partner with whom they have been constantly at odds. The reigning principle remains the same: adults need to be clear, firm, and in charge.

Single parenting does, however, entail unique challenges. Unless you are surrounded by an actively participating extended family or community, your parenting job lasts twenty-four hours a day, seven days a week, with no paid time off! Consequently, to avoid getting worn out, you'll need to take plenty of time to nurture yourself and refuel. Self-care for a parent, especially a single parent, is never a selfish act. On the contrary, it is a necessary ingredient of a healthy family life and hence one of the greatest gifts you can give to your kids.

Make sure you plan on some respite care in the first week of carrying out this program. Given that things typically get worse before they get better, you will need even more outside support than normal. When single parents don't have enough assistance or time off, it often makes it far more difficult to set limits when necessary with their kids. Even worse, when a parent relies too much on the kids for closeness or friendship, this new system can be difficult for everyone. Once you set and hold to the new limits, the kids will be upset and angry for a while. Prepare yourself for this initial turmoil. Think of it as a good sign that the kids trust your love enough to be mad at you.

It can also complicate the situation in a single parent household when children have been trying to fill the shoes of their missing parent. Sometimes children take on extra emotional or physical responsibilities even when mom or dad has not asked for this. At other times, a single parent has had to ask an older child to step up and carry more weight in a parent's absence.

Either way, even though taking on such added responsibility can be beneficial to both the child and the family, putting a child in a consistent parenting role also has distinct disadvantages. For example, a child deprived of age-appropriate activities can suffer significant social and emotional setbacks. If granted power over younger siblings, a child who acts like a parent also ends up bearing the brunt of sibling resentment and jealousy. In the final analysis, when it comes to setting limits, the adult should clearly be the one in charge, especially when instituting the Win-Win Way.

CHAPTER SEVENTEEN

NOT ALL CHILDREN ARE ALIKE

There are times as a parent when you realize that your job is not to be the parent you always imagined you'd be, the parent you always wished you had. Your job is to be the parent your child needs, given the particulars of his or her own life and nature.
-Ayelet Waldman

*N*ot all children will respond in the same way to their parents. In fact, one of the reasons you may be having more difficulty with one of your children is because of his or her inborn temperament. It's helpful to look at kids through this lens rather than thinking that one of your kids is "bad" or emotionally disturbed.

Researchers began to probe differences in children's temperaments through a longitudinal study begun in the 1950s. Since then, studies confirm that infants are born with certain built-in traits that affect their style of interacting with people, places and things throughout their lifetime.

This validates what many parents knew intuitively all along. Although raised in the same environment, children can have vastly different personality attributes. If not from birth, these differences can be quite apparent shortly thereafter, during the first year of life. Recent research is aimed at uncovering more of the specifics of genetically inherited traits.

Here are nine different factors as described by Chess and Thomas (1996) that can combine to define a child's temperament:

1. Activity levels: Is the child always moving or doing something or is he more mellow and relaxed?

2. Rhythmicity: Is the child regular in sleep and eating or more haphazard or difficult to get into a routine?

3. Approach/withdrawal: Does the child shy away from new people, places or activities or approach them willingly?

4. Adaptability: Does the child adjust to changes in plans or resist at times of transition?

5. Intensity: Does the child react strongly to situations, positively or negatively, with lots of intensity or react calmly and quietly?

6. Mood: Does the child more often express a negative or more positive attitude? Do the child's moods shift frequently or do they manifest in even-tempered behavior and a predictable frame of mind?

7. Persistence and attention span: Does the child give up quickly when frustrated with a task or keep on trying? Does the child stick with an activity for a long time or tend to get bored quickly?

8. Distractibility: Is the child easily distracted from what she's doing or does he shut out external distractions and stay with the activity?

9. Sensory threshold: Is the child bothered by stimuli such as loud noises, bright lights, smells, textures of food or clothing or does he/she tend to ignore them?

These nine traits combine in various ways to form three basic types of temperament. Approximately sixty-five percent of children fit one of the following three patterns; the other thirty-five percent are a combination of the three types. Understanding these patterns allows parents to tailor their responses to each child's personal characteristics. Within each temperament there are strengths and weaknesses. Working with rather than against a child's temperament is far more effective.

Easy or flexible children comprise about forty percent of all kids. These are the children that make parents feel like they are really competent as parents. These kids are generally happy, calm, and regular in sleep and eating, adaptable to change and not easily upset. The disadvantage of easy children is that they can pass "under the radar" of a parent who has another more difficult child who is taking lots of time and attention. Under those circumstances many parents carve out and schedule quality time with their easy child.

Difficult, active or feisty children are often high strung, intense, fearful of new people and situations, and easily upset by noise and commotion. They are often fussy and irregular in sleep and eating habits. Since they have difficulty transitioning from one activity to another, it helps to prepare them in advance for what is going to happen. These children need physical activities, exercise and vigorous play to work off their energy and frustrations.

Finding areas where they can have choices will help since they often say "no" reflexively before saying "yes." Luckily, this subgroup represents only about ten percent of all children because they often pose far more difficulties for caregivers. Not surprisingly, these are the children that are often referred for therapy, especially when there is a difficult match between parent and child. If you are reading this book, it is highly likely that one of your children has a more challenging temperament.

Slow to warm up or shy, cautious children represent about fifteen percent of the mix and are relatively inactive and fussy.

They tend to withdraw or to react negatively to new situations but gradually accommodate as they are exposed to the same people or places over time. They are calmed by sticking with a routine and need the patience of parents and teachers as they slowly develop their independence and confidence in new situations. Children with this temperament also can push back at parents' attempts to create and enforce rules and boundaries but for different reasons.

It is important to evaluate your own temperament and that of your partner as well. These nine traits provide insight for adult behavior too. With added perspective you'll be able to anticipate which kind of child will push your buttons. For example, if you are the "slow to warm up" type and you have a difficult, active child, your tendency may be to avoid that child. The difficult child will only redouble their efforts to get attention from you, which will inevitably backfire. The challenge for parents is to find effective ways to connect with each child while also being in charge and setting boundaries.

Understanding more about the unique characteristics of each of your children—and how they may differ from the kids of your sibs or close friends—will help you understand why certain kids require more consistent structure and limits to feel safe and secure in the world.

CHILDREN AND MENTAL ILLNESS

If this approach has not been effective, it is possible that your child may be suffering from a more serious problem and you need professional assistance. Even small children can begin to exhibit symptoms of attention deficit disorder, depression, anxiety disorders such as obsessive-compulsive behaviors, autism and autism spectrum disorders, childhood schizophrenia, or bipolar disorder.

Charles and Regina sought therapy for their 7-year-old son, Adam, who was having behavior problems both at home and at school. The couple also wanted marital help to improve their communication patterns. With two young children and two full time jobs, they had grown somewhat distant from one another and had years of stored upsets and resentments. The initial focus with this family was on the couple's issues, teaching them the "Repair Kit" (see Chapter 1 of *How's Your Family Really Doing?*) and helping them to become more of a team. Then we turned our attention to implementing the procedures of the Win-Win Way.

After a couple of months they reported only a 60% improvement in Adam's behavior. It was only after Adam was appropriately diagnosed and medicated for his attention deficit disorder that he finally showed dramatic improvement and could more easily respond to time outs and the star chart. Although many kids diagnosed with ADHD and other disorders can be helped without medication, sometimes the program is not enough by itself.

Some families need additional direction and supervision of an experienced mental health clinician or child and family therapist. Some parents are challenged by the extra needs of children who have been subjected to trauma such as domestic violence; victims of physical, emotional or sexual abuse; those born with fetal alcohol syndrome or addicted to drugs taken by their mother while in utero; or children adopted as toddlers or initially raised in environments lacking appropriate care and touch.

Although kids with more serious emotional problems typically benefit greatly from the loving implementation of clear boundaries, sometimes it is only with the help of adequate sleep, medication, dietary changes, and a more appropriate school setting that they can flourish. It is always a good idea to discuss your child's behaviors and issues with your pediatrician and to have your child evaluated if you suspect greater problems or if your child fits into any of the categories listed above.

GETTING PROFESSIONAL HELP WHEN NEEDED

If your efforts to achieve the desired changes in your family fail, it may be time to seek professional help. Most of us have the spirit of the Western cowboy or pioneer in us. We want to do things on our own, especially in relation to family or personal matters. Even when we're courageous enough to admit to having problems, we believe we should be able to work things out on our own. This myth of hard-nosed independence can be a tremendous asset. It can also be a detriment to our children's and our own best interests when consultation with friends or even some good therapy might help.

Remember that the best time to seek therapy is <u>before</u> small problems become big ones. This can save a lot of time, money and anguish in the long run. People often underestimate the seriousness of their situation and wait until everyday difficulties become a crisis. We encourage families to get "check-ups" for preventative mental health, especially if they have a question or discomfort about how someone in the family is doing. For your convenience, we have posted additional information about seeking a therapist on our website at **Strong-WilledChild.com**.

It may take a lot of support to unlearn old habits and it will certainly take time. Do you know other parents who have made positive changes with the same struggles? Most people who have the good fortune to live in healthy families have created them through hard work. Discuss with them how they achieved a healthier way of living, and look for guides to mentor you in this journey. Be gentle with yourself, your partner, and your children. Change can be difficult and scary. Celebrate the small steps along the way!

CHAPTER EIGHTEEN

CONCLUSION

We cannot always build the future for our youth,
but we can build our youth for the future.
-Franklin D. Roosevelt

*W*hen people are asked what they most value and cherish, the overwhelming majority say the same thing: their family. Parents are deeply committed to doing what is best for their children but, at the same time, may lack the knowledge or skills to do so. This can be particularly challenging when parenting bright, spirited, strong-willed children.

Raising kind and responsible children is no simple task, especially with kids who want to be the boss all the time. If we want our kids to have the grit necessary to be both happy and successful, it means teaching them to respect the needs of others, honor rules and limits, and learn self-control. In order to stem the growing tide of narcissism and entitlement, parents everywhere—not just those that go to counseling—need to know how to say no to their kids and really mean it.

We also need to dish out daily doses of love and warmth, learning to be five times more positive than negative. We need to say yes to their efforts, support their unique passions, and ask them to make age-appropriate contributions to both family and community. By learning how to create limits and respect that flows in both directions, our efforts can prevent the development of bigger, more difficult and dangerous problems in adolescence.

The modern world, with the demands of work, home, and the constant barrage of information coming at us from left and right, day and night, doesn't always support what's in the best interests of our children, our marriages or our communities. To build a better future, we must endow our young children with the social and emotional tools they need to survive life's inevitable stresses and frustrations.

Our book does not attempt to address the broader social issues that would provide more support to families—things like family leave, affordable housing and child care, livable wages, healthy food, physical education, and social and emotional education starting in pre-school. Our goal is to help parents, one family at a time, through giving them practical hands-on guidance to bring loving, effective discipline back into the home.

Let's start with our young children—before their patterns of behavior become bad habits. As we take on parental authority in a firm and loving manner or take it back after having lost it, our kids can go back to being kids again—relieved to let parents do their job of parenting. Kids who are raised to think of others as much as they think of themselves will better serve the world—and we certainly need them now more than ever.

Blog
References
Video Demos
Self-help Resources
Frequently Asked Questions

Can be found at:
Strong-WilledChild.com

CURRENT FAMILY ASSESSMENT

*B*egin by answering the fifty questions in the Current Family Assessment that follows. If you have a partner, a sibling or an older child who wants to participate, make copies of the test and complete it independently of one another. Hold off on discussions and comparisons for now.

This test is designed to work intimately with the content of *How's Your Family Really Doing? 10 Keys to a Happy Loving Family.* There are five questions that relate to each Key. Answer as honestly as you can. There are no right or wrong answers. The goal is to identify both strengths and areas for improvement in your family.

Each item in the assessment describes a particular behavior or attitude that might or might not accurately describe your family. You are scoring each item based on your unique personal perspective. Decide what you believe to be true about your family right now. For most people, the first step in any change process involves awareness. You will learn about elements of family functioning that you may not have thought about or put into words before.

If you prefer, you can download free 8 ½ x 11" copies
under "Forms" at **Strong-WilledChild.com**.

Current Family Assessment

This assessment contains fifty statements, each describing a particular family strength. How much improvement do you believe your family needs on each item? Grade from 1–5 according to the following scale:

1	2	3	4	5
much need for improvement		some need for improvement		no need for improvement

Key #1

____ We talk things over and know what's going on with each other.

____ Individuals speak for themselves, not for others.

____ Each family member finds a balance between talking and listening.

____ We notice and discuss some of the nonverbal messages we send and receive.

____ We listen to one another's ideas or points of view.

____ Subtotal **Key #1**

Key #2

____ Feelings are expressed in a balanced way—not too much or too little.

____ We comfort one another and are able to cry openly when sad.

____ Feelings of fear, frustration, and anger can be shared constructively.

____ As needed, we use calming methods such as centering and slow deep breaths.

____ We share more positive feelings (joy, tenderness, pleasure) than negative ones (fighting, criticizing, yelling, teasing).

____ Subtotal **Key #2**

Key #3

____ We recognize and encourage each other's unique strengths.

____ Mistakes are treated as helpful learning opportunities.

____ We adapt well to losses, changes, and transitions.

____ We have developed good habits of exercise, self-care, and regular sleep.

____ Each of us draws social support from friends, extended family, and social groups.

____ Subtotal **Key #3**

Key #4

___ We like to spend time together.
___ There are established routines for bedtime, meals, and family time.
___ Family meals taken together occur more than once a week.
___ We have rituals that are special to our family and/or extended family.
___ Each family member spends some quality time with every other member.

___ Subtotal **Key #4**

Key #5

___ Parenting of the children is not too soft but not too strict.
___ The parental figures in our family are on the same page and work together.
___ We use encouragement and praise far more often than negative words.
___ Punishment consists of consequences rather than spanking or yelling.
___ The children follow rules and respect the adults as the leaders of the family.

___ Subtotal **Key #5**

Key #6

___ We find a balance between closeness and distance with each other.
___ We feel close and connected to other family members *and* to friends.
___ There is overall respect for each other's needs for independence.
___ Family members are usually available to one another for help and support.
___ We have "boundaries" that provide privacy between adults and children.

___ Subtotal **Key #6**

Key #7

___ Differences among family members are acknowledged and valued.
___ People don't "need to be right," allowing others to have their own perspective.
___ We acknowledge and accept differences in temperament and learning style.
___ Parents focus on the strengths of individual differences and teach tolerance.
___ As appropriate, we state preferences and requests rather than making demands.

___ Subtotal **Key #7**

Key #8

___ We emphasize the positive aspects of situations rather than complaining.

___ We teach about social values and moral decision-making.

___ We treat others the way we would like to be treated.

___ We are capable of offering apologies and being forgiving.

___ We emphasize spiritual values, the bigger picture in life, and service to others.

___ Subtotal **Key #8**

Key #9

___ We negotiate and compromise rather than one person dominating decision-making.

___ We face problems early on rather than waiting until things get out of hand.

___ Parents are organized and provide leadership to make decisions and follow through.

___ Family members feel respected for their ideas even when they don't get their way.

___ Children are included in decision-making in a way that is age appropriate.

___ Subtotal **Key #9**

Key #10

___ Parents provide a model of love, respect, and healthy boundaries.

___ Parents walk their talk rather than falling back on "Do as I say, not as I do."

___ Criticism and defensiveness happen infrequently as forms of communication.

___ Parents work towards agreement and keep conflict away from the children.

___ Parents make their relationship a priority, cultivating friendship and intimacy.

___ Subtotal **Key #10**

___ Total **Keys #1-10**

ANALYZING YOUR ASSESSMENT

Add up your scores for each of the individual Keys. The maximum score for each Key is 25 points, so a comparison of the point scores for each Key will clearly highlight family strengths and areas for growth.

Chances are that Key #5 is problematic for you. Given the importance of teamwork, also look closely at your score on Key #10.

Besides noting these two specific keys, take a good look at other strengths and weaknesses. Examine your scores for each Key. Where did you score high? Where did you score poorly? If you have scored 16-25 on a Key, look on that component as a strength. If you scored from 12-15, the topics covered in this Key probably need some attention. A score from 5-11 identifies a problem Key. The results of this assessment will help you figure out where to direct your efforts toward change and whether or not you are ready to begin with the Win-Win Way.

Make sure to compare the scores you give your current family with those given by your partner or other family members. If there are big discrepancies, try to define what aspects of the Key led you to differing conclusions. Listen to the perspectives of others and explain how you see things. Obviously there is no "right" answer, so let it be okay to disagree. Bear in mind that each individual's experience will be unique, even being in the same family. If you remain open and curious, you can learn a lot about each other just by comparing notes. Some change will already begin to be seeded with this process.

If you have completed your analysis and figure out that you need family help, you can head in a few different directions. You might decide to read *How's Your Family Really Doing?* and give yourselves a tune-up before you try to implement the procedures in *Who's the Boss?* We particularly recommend Key #1, Talking and Listening, and Key #2, Expressing Feelings, because they are so important as foundations to healthy families. Most people need at least brushing up in these areas, and some need major overhauls.

FAMILY OF ORIGIN ASSESSMENT

The Family of Origin Assessment, for the family of your childhood, can help you to learn how your current family patterns may have been affected by past experiences. For scoring, if you grew up in more than one family for reasons of divorce, a loss in the family, or other reasons feel free to give separate scores for each. We have given you a couple of spaces on the assessment form to accommodate additional separate scores.

Similarly, if you have difficulty giving your family of origin just one score because things changed so much over time, make some chronological divisions and give separate scores for the different periods of time. (Example: "I really had two distinctly different families. The one while my dad was drinking and the one after he stopped.") Your earliest or more formative years, when you were living at home, are the most important part of our focus.

Turn to the next page and fill out the Family of Origin Assessment form. If you have a partner in this process, make copies of the test so you can fill it out independently from one another.

If you prefer, you can download free 8 ½ x 11" copies under "Forms" at **Strong-WilledChild.com**.

Family of Origin Assessment

This assessment contains fifty statements, each describing a particular family strength. Looking back, how much improvement do you believe the family of your childhood needed on each item? Grade from 1-5 according to the following scale:

1	2	3	4	5
much need for improvement		some need for improvement		no need for improvement

Family(s) of childhood

Key #1

___ ___ We talked things over and knew what was going on with each other.
___ ___ Individuals spoke for themselves, not for others.
___ ___ Each family member found a balance between talking and listening.
___ ___ We noticed and discussed some of the nonverbal messages we sent and received.
___ ___ We listened to one another's ideas or points of view.

___ ___ Subtotals **Key #1**

Key #2

___ ___ Feelings were expressed in a balanced way, not too much or too little.
___ ___ We comforted one another and were able to cry openly when sad.
___ ___ Feelings of fear, frustration, and anger were shared constructively.
___ ___ As needed, we used calming methods such as centering and slow deep breaths.
___ ___ We shared more positive feelings (joy, tenderness, pleasure) than negative ones (fighting, criticizing, yelling, teasing.)

___ ___ Subtotals **Key #2**

Key #3

___ ___ We recognized and encouraged each other's unique strengths.
___ ___ Mistakes were treated as helpful learning opportunities.
___ ___ We adapted well to losses, changes, and transitions.
___ ___ We practiced good habits of exercise, self-care, and regular sleep.
___ ___ Each of us drew social support from friends, extended family, and social groups.

___ ___ Subtotals **Key #3**

Key #4

___ ___ We liked to spend time together.

___ ___ There were established routines for bedtime, meals, and family time.

___ ___ Family meals together happened more than once a week.

___ ___ We had rituals that were special to our family and/or extended family.

___ ___ Each family member spent some quality time with every other member.

___ ___ Subtotals **Key #4**

Key #5

___ ___ My parents were not too soft but not too strict.

___ ___ My parents were on the same page about how to parent the children.

___ ___ My parents used encouragement and praise far more often than negative words.

___ ___ Punishment consisted of consequences rather than spanking or yelling.

___ ___ The children followed rules and respected the adults as the leaders of the family.

___ ___ Subtotals **Key #5**

Key #6

___ ___ We had a healthy balance between closeness and distance with each other.

___ ___ We felt close and connected to other family members *and* to friends.

___ ___ There was overall respect for each other's needs for independence.

___ ___ Family members were usually available to one another for help and support.

___ ___ We had "boundaries" that provided privacy between adults and children.

___ ___ Subtotals **Key #6**

Key #7

___ ___ Differences among family members were acknowledged and valued.

___ ___ People didn't "need to be right," allowing others to have their own perspective.

___ ___ My parents acknowledged and accepted differences in temperament and learning style.

___ ___ My parents focused on the strengths of individual differences and taught us tolerance.

___ ___ As appropriate, we stated preferences and requests rather than making demands.

___ ___ Subtotals **Key #7**

Key #8

___ ___ We emphasized the positive aspects of situations rather than complaining.

___ ___ My parents taught about social values and moral decision-making.

___ ___ We treated others the way we wanted to be treated.

___ ___ We were capable of offering apologies and being forgiving.

___ ___ We valued spiritual ideas, the bigger picture in life, and service to others.

___ ___ Subtotals **Key #8**

Key #9

___ ___ We negotiated and compromised rather than one person dominating decision-making.

___ ___ We faced problems early on rather than waiting until things got out of hand.

___ ___ My parents were organized and provided leadership in making decisions.

___ ___ Family members felt respected for their ideas even when they didn't get their way.

___ ___ Parents included children in decision-making in an age-appropriate way.

___ ___ Subtotals **Key #9**

Key #10

___ ___ My parents provided a model of love, respect, and healthy boundaries.

___ ___ My parents walked their talk rather than falling back on "Do as I say, not as I do."

___ ___ Criticism and defensiveness happened only infrequently as forms of communication.

___ ___ My parents worked toward agreement and kept conflict away from the children.

___ ___ My parents made their relationship a priority, cultivating friendship and intimacy.

___ ___ Subtotals **Key #10**

___ ___ Total **Keys #1-10**

COMPARING ASSESSMENTS

If you haven't already done so, go to Appendix A and complete and tabulate your scores for your **Current Family Assessment**, circling the Keys that you think might need some attention. Also look at any particular questions for which you scored poorly, even if your overall score for that key was good. (Reminder: If you scored 16-25 points on a Key, see it as an area of strength. If you scored from 12-15, this Key probably needs some attention. If you scored from 5-11, you have identified a significant problem Key.)

Following this same process, now tabulate your scores and review your **Family of Origin Assessment**. Notice any similarities or differences between your family of origin and current family. Have any of your buttons been pushed? Does your current family have similar trouble spots or have you left old patterns behind? If you see generational improvement, give yourself a pat on the back. You've probably already done some good work. If not, those keys can become target areas for growth and change.

Now looking more in depth at your family of origin assessment, have you unknowingly overcompensated for past weaknesses? Since we are looking most closely at Key #5, reflect on what kind of discipline your parents used to raise you. As we discussed previously, we typically either imitate our parenting models or rebel against them, going in the opposite direction. Parents who were raised with too much harshness, were spanked a lot, or received little praise, often become too permissive with their own kids. Many people compensate too much and need to come back to a point of greater balance.

Now reflect on your answers to Key #10. Have you unknowingly replicated the same kind of relationship with your partner that was modeled by your mom and dad? Or conversely, do you find yourself compensating too much for what you saw and didn't want to re-create? These are the important elements to evaluate as you put the magnifying glass to current and past patterns. The results of these assessments ideally help direct your efforts towards change. Rather than judge yourself or your parenting partner too harshly, be sure to look at your strengths and also to congratulate yourselves and each other for having the courage to face these issues. As you make the changes in your parenting style and strengthen your teamwork with your partner, you are breaking your bondage to the past and creating new, more loving patterns for future generations.

NOTES:

ACKNOWLEDGMENTS

*T*he approach described in this book began over forty years ago. Needless to say, the material has gone through thousands of permutations and augmentations through the years. When clients come in distress over the challenges their families are facing, we feel a great sense of compassion. We have also felt a sense of responsibility for finding meaningful and effective solutions to their problems.

This "project," (because it is so much more than a book) crystallized with the help and support of so many dear friends, family and colleagues. We want first to give heartfelt thanks for the editorial assistance of Noah Brand, Kjell Rudestam, and members of our staff. Each had an amazing ability to climb into our vision and help sort through a maze of possible presentation options. We also want to thank the many mentors in our lives who have paved the way, taught and encouraged us, including Virginia Satir, Salvador Minuchin, Charlie Fishman, Larry and Evelyn Thomas, Ron Taffel, Robert Brooks, Ram Dass, Brother David Steindl-Rast, Jordan Paul and Maurice Elias.

We have deep love and appreciation for the whole staff of the Family Therapy Institute of Santa Barbara. Extraordinarily loyal and committed, several of our staff have given decades of invaluable support and fodder for our thinking. Our board of directors, equally loyal, has provided unwavering assistance throughout this time.

We give special thanks to each of our moms for continuing to grow, thrive, and be happy through loss and changes aplenty. We are grateful for your ideas, editorial inputs, and the encouragement to chase our dreams.

We also appreciate the many families and individuals we have treated but who have been such a "treat" to us in return. They have shared their hearts and souls and stories in a way that has helped us to refine our thinking and approaches at least a zillion times. They have shown us where we have gotten stuck, and taught us how to move on.

Finally, we would really like to acknowledge each other. We feel immensely proud and happy that we are alive and more in love each day. We have survived and thrived through the rigors of writing this book, through tons of work and countless, precious moments of teasing, prodding, supporting, and debating.

As for the tools that we have shared in these pages, the proof of the pudding is in our ability to co-create so many wonderful gifts throughout our marriage: the Institute that we direct, the two houses we have built, and the fine young men that our sons have become. We want to thank Sean and Cree for being our very best students and teachers, and for finally getting over thinking that it was the worst thing in the world to have two shrinks for parents. We feel blessed to welcome our daughter-in-law, Gillian, into our lives, as well as our new and first grandchild, Avery.

ABOUT THE AUTHORS

$\mathscr{D}$on and Debra are a team both at home and at the office. Husband and wife for over thirty years, they have simultaneously served as directors of the Family Therapy Institute of Santa Barbara, a nonprofit organization. In this capacity they oversee the clinical work of fourteen therapists providing help to hundreds of clients each year. They are authors and coauthors of numerous articles on parenting and clinical issues. In 2009, Don won the title of "Best Family Therapist" in a poll taken by SBParent.com. In 2010, Debra was honored with an Award for Service to the Community by local therapists and the Mayor of Santa Barbara "for 30 years of inspiration, leadership, and training provided to thousands of clinicians, and the devotion exemplified with consistent visionary work for the community."

Don has a bachelor's degree from Dartmouth, a masters in school-child psychology from University of Virginia, and a Ph.D. in clinical psychology from California School of Professional Psychology. Also a musician, he was songwriter and music director for the animated PBS hit, *Jay Jay the Jet Plane*. His public education efforts have culminated in the writing and production of *Happy Kids Songs*, a series of songs and activities that help young children with social and emotional learning. His music has won over ten major awards.

Debra received her undergraduate degree in psychology with distinction from Stanford University and her masters in social welfare from University of California at Berkeley with a specialty in family therapy and community mental health. Prior to founding the Institute in 1979, she was the Executive Director of Social Advocates for Youth in the San Francisco Bay Area, working with runaway teens and children at risk. She has taught marriage and family therapy at Antioch University, Pacifica Graduate Institute, numerous local agencies, schools and mental health facilities. She finds respite from her busy life through painting, hiking and being with her much loved dog, Shammy.

Don and Debra have lived in Santa Barbara, Ca., for the past thirty-six years. They share a love of games, music, movies, biking, hiking, travel, and art.

Don and Debra are available for lectures, keynote presentations and workshops that range from a few hours to a few days, either as co-presenters or as individuals. They offer workshops to the general public, teachers and mental health professionals.

They have provided advanced training, consultation and supervision for over 30 years. They consult with non-profit counseling centers, medical, legal and law enforcement agencies, private businesses and individuals.

Areas of expertise include systems analysis, law and ethics, on-site case consultation, social and emotional learning, and training in specific topics regarding work with couples, families, teens and children.

Other Great Materials by Don MacMannis, Ph.D. (a.k.a. Dr. Mac)

Happy Kids Songs.com
by Dr. Mac & Friends

Award-winning PBS songwriter.

Fun and fabulous, adult-quality music with a message!

Happy Kids' Songs Workbook: Hands-on Activities for Social, Emotional and Character Development
This 125-page activity book includes the kids' lyrics and coloring pages from all 8 of the albums plus adds more than a hundred lessons and activities for parents and teachers to share with kids.

8 Great Themes:

Friends & Sharing
Social Skills & Bullying
Feelings & Fears
Practice & Success
Talking & Listening
Manners & Character
Happiness & Attitude
Respect & Responsibility

"I highly recommend this creative and entertaining way to give children life-long tools for getting along. Fabulous full-production music for the souls of children and families."
– Jack Canfield, Co-Author, *Chicken Soup for the Soul®*

Listen to samples at HappyKidsSongs.com

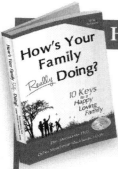

How's Your Family Really Doing?

10 Keys to a Happy Healthy Family

2012 Eric Hoffer Award
2012 Book of the Year Award, <u>ForeWord</u> Magazine

Excellent, informative, helpful, and well-written in a reader-friendly manner that will be read and r e-read by families and professionals alike."
-Robert Brooks, Ph.D., Psychologist, Faculty of Harvard Medical School, Co-author of *Raising Resilient Children*, and *The Power of Resilience"*

"... a resource that will be of lasting value to parents, prospective parents, grandparents, and clinicians. It is welcoming, warm, and wise."

-Maurice J. Elias, Ph.D., Director of Clinical Training, Rutgers University
Co-author, *Emotionally Intelligent Parenting*

"Debra and Don have dedicated enormous time and effort to separating myth from fact. In a few minutes, one learns which of the 10 Keys need more attention and exactly why. The average person would have to commit great resources in time and expense securing this specific kind of family relationship-assessment! How's Your Family Really Doing? offers basic tools to create happiness in family life upon which we can build a unique home, one in which we can live and love each other for many years to come—really!"

-From the foreword by Ron Taffel, Ph.D., Author of *Childhood Unbound*

- **Learn from research about successful relationships.**
- **Assess your family with a 50-point self-evaluation.**
- **Strengthen your skills with dozens of tips and tools.**
- **Identify and overcome the effects of past influences.**

HowsYourFamily.com

Made in the USA
San Bernardino, CA
12 May 2019